The Meaningful Money Retirement Guide

The Meaningful Money Retirement Guide

Everything You Need to Know and Do for a Secure and Happy Retirement

Pete Matthew

 Harriman House

HARRIMAN HOUSE LTD
3 Viceroy Court
Bedford Road
Petersfield
Hampshire
GU32 3LJ
GREAT BRITAIN
Tel: +44 (0)1730 233870

Email: enquiries@harriman-house.com
Website: harriman.house

First published in 2025 by Harriman House, an imprint of Pan Macmillan
EU Representative: Macmillan Publishers Ireland Limited, 1st Floor, The Liffey Centre, 117-126 Sherriff Street Upper, Dublin 1, D01 YC45
Associated companies throughout the world
www.panmacmillan.com

Copyright © Pete Matthew 2025

The right of Pete Matthew to be identified as the author has been asserted in accordance with the Copyright, Design and Patents Act 1988.

Paperback ISBN: 978-1-80409-065-7
eBook ISBN: 978-1-80409-066-4

British Library Cataloguing in Publication Data
A CIP catalogue record for this book can be obtained from the British Library.

All rights reserved. No part of this publication may be reproduced, stored in a retrieval system, or transmitted in any form or by any means (including without limitation electronic, mechanical, photocopying, recording, or otherwise) without the prior written permission of the publisher. This book is sold subject to the condition that it shall not, by way of trade or otherwise, be lent, hired out, or otherwise circulated without the publisher's prior consent. This work is reserved from text and data mining (Article 4(3) Directive (EU) 2019/790).

Harriman House does not have any control over, or any responsibility for, any author or third-party websites (including without limitation URLs, emails and QR codes) referred to in or on this book. This book is for informational purposes only. Readers are advised to consult an appropriate professional in light of their relevant circumstances and requirements before acting on any information in this book.

No responsibility or liability for loss occasioned to any person or corporate body acting or refraining to act as a result of reading material in this book can be accepted by the publisher, by the author, or by the employers of the author.

Printed and bound by CPI Group (UK) Ltd.

Having a supportive family provides an incredible foundation on which to build good things. They will encourage you when you're feeling low and bring you down a peg or two when you get too big for your boots. They will ground you.

Best of all, a loving family provides a refuge when life becomes overwhelming. You can head home, shut the world out and just be, knowing that those around you have your back, no matter what.

I am blessed beyond measure that both my Matthew family and my Jackson in-laws embody these values. Without fail they have loved me throughout my life; there's no way I could do half of what I do without their support.

My beautiful girls are the most precious things in the world to me. My wife of 27 years, Joanne, and my daughters, Ellie and Kate – without you I am nothing.

This book is dedicated to my whole family, whom I love with all my heart.

Oh, and our dogs Maisy and Callie insisted I mention them here too, so there you are.

Contents

Acknowledgements ix

Introduction 1

Chapter 1: What Is Retirement? 7
Chapter 2: Cash Flow Is Everything 13
Chapter 3: The Three Phases Of Retirement 19

Phase 1: The Home Straight 23

Chapter 4: Making Plans 27
Chapter 5: Taking Stock 35
Chapter 6: The UK State Pension 43
Chapter 7: How Defined Benefit Pensions Work 49
Chapter 8: How Defined Contribution Pensions Work 59
Chapter 9: Everything That *Isn't* A Pension 73
Chapter 10: Positioning The Pieces 89
Chapter 11: Catching Up 107

Phase 2: The Great Transition 115

Chapter 12: The Danger Zone 119
Chapter 13: Optimising Cash Flow 131

Chapter 14: Investing Options	139
Chapter 15: The Cash Flow Ladder	149
Chapter 16: Managing Spending Patterns	163

Phase 3: The New Normal — **169**

Chapter 17: Settling In For The Long Haul	173
Chapter 18: Reviewing Your Plans	179
Chapter 19: Later Life Planning	189
Chapter 20: Estate Planning	203
Chapter 21: Conclusion – A Meaningful Retirement	219
How I can help you further	221
Endnotes	223

Acknowledgements

I often get asked how I get everything done. I'm always surprised by this because I don't think I'm really any more productive than anyone else. I usually answer by saying that I don't watch much TV, but in reality it's because I have great people around me.

My 'day job' is serving as the CEO of Jacksons in Penzance. We're 21 people working with brilliant clients to deliver financial planning that enables them to live their lives well. The team are all superb, a joy to lead and endlessly supportive and grounding.

Special mention should go to my business partners Mike Caffry and Chas Cox, who have always been encouraging of my 'distracting hobby' at Meaningful Money and kept me focused when necessary. Also, credit goes to Sharon Bray, my Practice Manager, who has brought so much of my vision into reality because she just gets stuff done. Not only that, Sharon is a visionary herself and we're entirely aligned on what we want to build in the coming decade. I feel blessed beyond measure to have found such an exceptional person with whom to do great work.

On the Meaningful Money side, my podcast co-host and best friend in the world, Roger Weeks, makes producing the show a joy. We just laugh at each other throughout and, it turns out, the audience love his gentle Cornish voice more than they do mine! Thanks for giving me your time, Rog – love you, man.

Nick Mitchell is the gift that keeps on giving. He's responsible for manning the email inbox, fielding the (many) Meaningful Academy support requests, researching for the podcasts and moderating the Facebook groups (ably assisted there by the inimitable Ruth Bell). I couldn't do this without your help Nick, and I'm very grateful.

And then there's my right-hand man, Kaloyan Tsilev. I was introduced to Kal by our mutual friend Chris Marr and we hit it off straightaway. Since then, Kal has become far more than a video editor, as skilled as he is at that work. He's a strategic partner, challenging me to think and dream bigger, and then working back from there to give me the next thing I need to do to move us towards our goals. Without him, the YouTube channel wouldn't have exploded these past few years, Meaningful Academy would still be something 'I'd like to do one day' and the Facebook community and email digest wouldn't have happened at all. Kal – you're a legend, and I love working with you. Here's to even greater things in future and a lifelong friendship.

To Craig Pearce and the whole team at Harriman House, thank you for your patience and encouragement throughout the process of getting this book ready. You know that I found this one harder than the first, but without you guys it wouldn't have happened at all, and I'm grateful for that.

Of course, all this would be for nothing if no one was watching, listening or reading. So to you, the Meaningful Money audience – thank you for your engagement, challenge and encouragement. You're the reason I keep going and plan to do so for a long time yet.

Introduction

IT WAS ABOUT SIX WEEKS after we finished working for Steve and Jane that they called and dropped the bombshell: "We've both decided to retire. Today. Five years early."

A few weeks earlier, we had completed their financial plan, stress-tested it and made recommendations. As DIY investors aged around 60, Steve and Jane were delighted that all the effort they had put in over their working lives had put them in such a strong position.

They had intended retiring at age 65, but when we spoke, it was clear that they were flagging at work, going through the motions and biding their time. What they really wanted to do was buy a campervan and drive around Europe.

Through the planning work we did together, we were able to reassure them that rather than grinding out five more years in jobs they had come to resent, they could in fact retire early and start living out their dreams right away.

Like so many clients, they struggled to believe this at first, but in the six weeks since we completed our planning work, they had clearly been thinking more about it. Steve relayed the story to me:

> I'd had a rubbish morning at work and so I called Jane at lunchtime to whinge about it. I said to her that in light of the work we'd done with Jacksons,[1] I was seriously thinking about handing in my notice. In the next breath, Jane told me that she'd just done exactly that about ten minutes before I'd called. I hung up and went and drafted my retirement letter to my boss! Thank you for making it possible…

My first response to news like this is always a quiet voice saying, 'I hope I got my numbers right!' I mean, these people had made the biggest financial decision of their lives on the basis of my calculations! This quickly passed, of course, because we do check these things *very* carefully!

My second response was delight. I was so happy that Steve and Jane were able to embark on the next exciting phase of their lives together, and five years earlier than they had hoped.

Make no mistake, Steve and Jane had done the work to get themselves into this position. My only role was to provide some validation and encouragement that they had done everything necessary to retire well.

Like so many people I have met throughout my career, Steve and Jane had consistently made good decisions about their finances. They weren't genius investors, and they weren't given a leg up by an inheritance or a lottery win. They were middle-income, hard-working people who understood what needed to be done to get themselves in a position where working was optional.

I believe that anyone can achieve the same outcome. The main thing that holds so many of us back is an ignorance of how the personal finance system works. It can all seem so overwhelming that it's easier to do nothing and bury our heads in the sand.

My first book, *The Meaningful Money Handbook*, was published in September 2018. It is designed to be the one book that anyone based in the UK can read to understand everything they need to KNOW and everything they need to DO to put their finances on a firm footing.

That book covers the basics of budgeting and debt elimination, protecting against unforeseen life events with insurance and how to build wealth by investing for the long term.

This is the stuff we still don't teach well enough in school and yet affects every single one of us. I haven't had to solve a quadratic equation once since I left college, and yet I've had to manage my

Introduction

money every day since getting my first job. So why don't we teach our children how to do that?

All the subjects I covered in that book – the day-to-day basics of financial management – serve a future purpose: one day, most of us will either want or need to stop working, and most of us couldn't live on just the state pension.

And so we need to forgo some spending today in order to set aside money that we can spend when that time comes. In short, we invest now so that we can RETIRE one day.

The first book stopped short of talking much about retirement, and so this book picks up where that one left off.

The everything you need to KNOW and everything you need to DO structure has served me well for years on the Meaningful Money podcast, which now has over 500 episodes and over seven million downloads.

It was also the broad structure for most of the chapters in the first book and I'll carry it over for this book, too. Each chapter will set the context in the 'KNOW' section and then follow up with practical steps in the 'DO' section.

Stepping back and viewing the book as a whole, first we need to lay some foundations. We need to talk about what it means to retire and why I believe that the fundamental success factor for anyone looking to retire well is a mastery of cash flow, that is, money in and money out, income and expenses.

Throughout the rest of the book, together we will walk through each of the three phases of retirement:

1. **The Home Straight.** This is the five- to ten-year period before we make the leap into retirement. We need to answer some important questions here, like do I have enough? Is the money I do have in the right places? How do I get money out of my pensions after all these years of putting money in? Together we will work out exactly what all the hard work you have done

while you have been working will amount to in retirement, and how to really sprint towards the line and make the most of your later working years.

2. **The Great Transition.** This is when we press the button on our plans and start to move into retirement itself. It's also the point at which we start drawing down from our investments and pensions, which usually means a change in the way that money is invested. We'll talk about how to optimise all of this in a way which is easy for you to manage. For some, retirement is a cliff-edge point in time, for others a transition over months or years. But for everyone, it's a sea change in perspective and experienced reality.

3. **The New Normal.** That sea change becomes the day-to-day pretty quickly though! As we groove into our new life, we need to maintain our financial plans so that they continue to provide for our needs. So we'll talk about how to review our finances effectively and how to adjust as our circumstances inevitably change throughout retirement. And of course, as we get older, our minds eventually turn to what happens when we're no longer around, so we need to talk about estate planning, long-term care and how to leave things in a good state for the next generation.

By the time we're done, we should have covered everything you need to KNOW and everything you need to DO to set yourself up for a secure and happy retirement.

Sound like a plan? Excellent – let's crack on…

Chapter 1
What Is Retirement?

RETIREMENT IS A TRICKY SUBJECT to cover because it means something different to everyone. If you do a Google images search for retirement, you'll see lots of stereotypical couples holding hands while walking along a beach in the sunshine.

I live near the beach, so I did that yesterday (except it was raining), and I'm nowhere near retirement! So it seems odd that this would be the visual archetype for a happy and fulfilled retirement.

It's impossible to fully separate the idea of retirement from stopping work, but really, they're not necessarily linked. For me, I have no plans to stop work, ever. Oh, it'll change form and frequency for sure, but doing *nothing*? That's unimaginable to me.

If you can break the link in your mind between retirement and stopping working, right here at the start of our journey together, I think it'll help you.

Part of the problem with the word 'retirement' is its historical connotations.

Retirement ain't what it used to be

Not that long ago, the norm was that we would work our entire lives for one employer. We would retire after 40+ years with a handshake from the boss, some warm words and a carriage clock, and then we'd enjoy a period of inactive dotage funded by a guaranteed pension while we waited for death.

I don't know about you, but that doesn't fill me with excitement! Mercifully, things are very different now.

Guaranteed, employer-sponsored pensions are much rarer than they used to be, so these days, most of us have to take retirement funding into our own hands.

People are living longer than they did in the past and we're enjoying better health, so we're likely to be retired for much longer. That means we will need more money set aside to pay for this and we're likely to want to fill that extra time with meaningful pursuits.

And yet still, I think that what most people have in mind when they hear the word retirement is this: stop work > do nothing > wait to die.

Thank goodness it *has* changed!

The FIRE movement

Taking things to the other extreme, sometime in the 2010s there appeared the inexorable rise of the Financial Independence Retire Early (FIRE) movement. One of the leading proponents of this was Mr Money Mustache,[2] but the whole idea has really caught on now, particularly with younger Gen X and Millennials.

The catchy acronym and the obvious appeal of retiring early has, I'm sure, been a factor in the rise in the popularity of this approach, but actually, Mr Money Mustache would say that FIRE doesn't have anything to do with stopping work at all. Instead it means:

Complete freedom to be the best, most powerful, energetic, happiest and most generous version of You that you can possibly be.[3]

Now that I can get on board with.

Some FIRE followers go hardcore, saving huge percentages of their income and living like monks so that they can amass enough to retire very early, even as young as their 30s. Others take a more laid-back approach where it isn't just about achieving FI, but enjoying the journey too.

Freedom. Choice. That's what I would consider retirement to be – not having to work if we don't want to.

For many of us, work in some form will be a large part of our retirement plans. That work may be paid or voluntary. The routine of work and its physical demands can be good for us, helping us to retain mental and bodily resilience for longer. There's no doubt that a lifetime of work followed by doing absolutely nothing is a sure way to an early grave.

Phasing into retirement

These days, many more of us ease into retirement over time. This takes two main forms: either we reduce the number of hours we work per week, or we take work which is less stressful than we're used to.

At the latter end of our careers, many of us are at the highest point of our earnings power, and with more money usually comes more responsibility and stress.

If we can gradually enter the next stage of life by going a bit easier on ourselves, then it makes sense to me. It allows us to get used to the idea of backing off a bit and may allow our workplace to get used to doing without us too.

Phasing into retirement also means that we don't have to draw so much from our accumulated capital, or trigger pensions quite so early as we might if we came to a hard stop. We can also get used to living on a bit less income, which is likely to be the case when and if we *fully* retire.

Mini retirements

Another lifestyle I'm seeing more and more people talk about is the idea of a series of mini retirements. Here, we could save money for a few years with the intention of taking a long-term break from work, perhaps six months or even a year or two. Maybe we could travel, do some volunteering, or just take an extended break from work. Perhaps we could use the time to retrain and pursue a different career when we return to work.

I remember being trained as an adviser to refer to retirement as "the longest holiday" in a naff sales technique designed to get people excited about saving for it. This is still a view that has retirement as a future aim, though. The mini-retirement approach seeks to enjoy the benefits of retirement in piecemeal form throughout life – an attractive idea, I'd say.

Retirement is yours to define

However you choose to structure your life and your eventual retirement, the mechanics are largely the same. Mostly it comes down to how we are going to pay our expenses while taking some time for ourselves. Each of the options above are just variations on the themes that we'll discuss as we go through this book.

One thing that I always say to clients is that we should start with what we want to happen. What's the dream? If we could design our perfect life, what would that look like?

Then we work back from there and see if we can realistically achieve

Chapter 1: What Is Retirement?

those goals within the timescales we're hoping for and within the constraints of the UK personal finance and tax system.

If it turns out that our dreams are completely unrealistic, then we'll need to reassess things, but I find that most people have the common sense to realise that they're not going to retire as millionaires if they only save £50 a month.

So as we're going through this, I want to encourage you to dream big, while keeping your feet firmly on the ground.

Remember this is your retirement and your life. It is yours to design as you want.

Chapter 2
Cash Flow Is Everything

IF I HAD TO DISTIL personal financial planning down to one core truth, the one thing that underpins all financial success, it would be this:

> Spend less than you earn.

Indeed, the first third of my previous book was dedicated to exactly this subject. And it remains true in retirement, even if it may look a bit different from when we're building wealth.

Cash flow is the right expression for this – it's the flow of cash through our hands: money in and money out.

When we're building wealth, we earn money from a job or from self-employment. We may also receive income from investments, such as rent from a second property or dividends from a share portfolio that we've built.

If we're going to build wealth at all, we need to spend less than is coming in and put some money away. Then we need to invest that spare money so that it grows, maintaining its real value so that we can spend it in later life.

In the traditional retirement, we're now in a position where there is no earned income coming in anymore. We'll likely have pensions, and those other income sources should continue too, as they're not dependent on whether we're working or not. But many of us spend more than our income in retirement, which means that we will need to dip into capital.

And that's fine, as long as that capital doesn't run out. If it does, then we may run into trouble.

A spending timeline

Let's consider the timeline of a typical person, from the point at which we get our first job.

This can be a very challenging time financially, as this is likely the lowest salary we'll ever receive. If we're still living with family, then costs will be low and we will be able to save, as long as we are disciplined to do so. (I don't charge my girls rent or board, as long as they can show me that they are saving at least half their income.)

But when we leave home and are responsible for rent or a mortgage, plus all the associated bills of running a household, then money can get really tight.

Hopefully, over time, we will receive promotions or move into different jobs that pay better. If we can minimise the insidious increase in spending that often accompanies a rising salary, sometimes known as lifestyle creep, then life will get a little easier over time.

Maybe kids come along, and with them 20 odd years of paying for pretty much everything! For many women, particularly, there may be years of earning nothing at all, which has a big impact on their personal financial situation, something we'll address later on.

And then the children fly the nest, by which time we are likely in our late 40s or even well into our 50s (or 60s!). Now we experience our peak earning years, rising to the higher levels of our chosen career and receiving the salary to go with it.

At the same time, our costs may be starting to reduce. Perhaps we have paid off our mortgage, releasing a large amount of disposable income each month. Generally we will be free of other debt and should be saving aggressively as the finish line of retirement starts to become visible on the horizon.

And then we retire, and the reverse is true. Now we're earning little or nothing, and our costs haven't reduced much at all from when we were earning well. There may be a period before all our pensions kick in where we will need to draw heavily on our capital.

Before too long, spending finds a level, all the pensions have started, and things settle down. Eventually, as we age, we will have less energy to travel and we'll find that we have all the stuff we need around us. And so we find that our spending actually starts to fall as we move through retirement into our later years.

And then the spectre of long-term care may appear, where costs will increase astronomically. The house may be sold to pay for it and, eventually, the Reaper calls and our time is up.

Our spending rises and falls, and so does our income, depending on our time of life. Preparing well for retirement is about maximising the flow of money into our retirement savings when we can.

Retirement cash flow

If the maxim 'spend less than you earn' underpins all financial success, as I posited at the start of this chapter, then how does this apply to retirement, when we're almost certain to be spending *more* than we earn?

We need to expand our understanding of the word 'earn'. If we stop working altogether in retirement then we won't be earning anything directly. But we may be receiving income from pensions that we earned earlier in our career.

We may also be earning income from our accumulated investments or property.

Most of us will need to dip into capital to a greater or lesser extent when we retire. That's fine of course – it's the reason we set that money aside in the first place! As long as we're careful not to spend all our savings and investments too quickly, then we can call these withdrawals earnings too.

In retirement, then, 'spend less than you earn' becomes the far less catchy:

> Manage your spending at a level that, if it exceeds your guaranteed income, doesn't erode your capital too quickly.

There are two elements to this:

1. The first is that we can't really get away from the need to manage our spending. Most of us will never be able to throw all caution to the wind and spend whatever we like, because our incomes and capital just won't sustain it. If we change the Bentley every other year, we're going to burn through our capital pretty quickly! This is going to require some form of ongoing budgeting.

2. Second, we need to manage our capital. Note that I don't say *maintain* our capital. It is quite acceptable, desirable even, to erode our capital to enjoy life to the full. We just need to ensure we don't spend it all too quickly – we don't want our money to run out before we do.

This is cash flow planning in retirement – we manage spending and we manage our capital. In a nutshell, that's what this book is designed to help you achieve.

Long-term care

We'll discuss long-term care in more detail later in the book, but I wanted to just briefly mention it here.

There's no escaping the fact that if we need long-term residential care in later life, all cash flow bets are off. I don't want to be fatalistic

Chapter 2: Cash Flow Is Everything

because this is something that still won't affect the majority of us, but the average cost of a residential care home in the UK is £3,290 per month, rising to £4,160 per month if you add in nursing care.[4] And that's the average – it's quite easy to spend significantly more than that, depending on where you live in the UK.

This will have a significant impact on the finances of most retirees, of course, but may not be as bad as we fear. I see many retired couples curtailing their spending while in their earlier retirement years because they fear that they may need long-term care in the future. I think that's a shame, not least because they often leave too much money on the table when they could have been enjoying it in their earlier retirement years. A recurring theme throughout this book will be that if you are forced to make a choice, you should prioritise the present over the future. In practice, though, life is rarely that binary.

For those over age 65, only about one in four people needs help with at least one activity of daily living. In other words, they need some form of help from a carer, whether paid or unpaid. For those over 80, that rises to one in two.[5]

Of those in residential care, the life expectancy (and hence the overall amount of money that will be paid in fees) predictably reduces the older you are when entering care. Life expectancy for a 65-year-old female in care is about seven years, and just over six years for a male. At age 80, that falls to 4.2 years for females and 3.1 years for males.[6]

All this is to say that the majority of us will not need care at all, and if we need the most expensive form of care, it likely won't be for a long time. Maybe the spectre of care fees isn't quite so scary as we first thought?

And if this is true, then maybe we should focus more on the spending patterns earlier in retirement and enjoy our best years more?

Before we get into the meat of the book, I want to discuss the three main phases of a classical retirement. That's the next chapter.

Chapter 3
The Three Phases Of Retirement

AS I'VE MENTIONED PREVIOUSLY, GONE are the days – for most of us at least – where retirement is a hard stop, where one day we're working and the next day we're retired.

But even if that is your experience, you will be thinking about and preparing for retirement for several years before it comes… or you should be.

Over my 25 years of advising clients, I've identified three distinct stages of the retirement journey.

Let's look at these briefly now. They'll then form the structure for the rest of the book.

Phase 1: The Home Straight

Many clients first present to a financial adviser at the beginning of this stage. They will say words to the effect, 'We want to understand what everything we've accumulated adds up to, and what it might mean for us one day when we come to retire.'

They are rounding the final bend in their work-race and they can see the finish line ahead. They are nearly at the end of their journey and they want to give it one last push to finish strongly. They are still thinking in terms of 'one day', but that day is coming ever closer – they're on the Home Straight.

For some this is a three-year period, but for most it is longer than that, between five and ten years. This is a time of getting to grips with the money you have saved so far, how much it is worth and what kind of lifestyle it might provide for you. And it's a time for maximising our efforts in the last few years to make the picture as rosy as it can be.

Part of this phase is understanding how everything works: the mechanics of things like pension crystallisation and withdrawal, the taxation of different sources of income, different allowances and the like. We haven't had to understand these up to now as we've just been saving and investing. Now our minds turn to disinvesting and spending.

People often use this phase as an opportunity to tidy things up and simplify their pension plans to make their lives easier when the time comes to retire. I call this 'positioning the pieces', and it is best done with plenty of time to spare. Everything needs to be thought through well in advance so there won't be any surprises… good or bad!

In this section we'll talk about how the different kinds of UK pension work, including the state pension, as well as all the other kinds of investments that you might hold, from ISAs to investment bonds. When you know what you're dealing with, you can start to think about how to make the best of what you have built.

Phase 2: The Great Transition

Eventually we'll press the button and step over the line into retirement, however we have defined that for ourselves. It may be a one-and-done thing, or we may begin the process of transitioning to our new lives over a period of time.

We may trigger income and tax-free cash from pensions, perhaps, or start drawing from our cash reserves or from our ISAs. Perhaps the state pension will kick in, depending on when we have chosen to retire.

We will start our new daily routines, perhaps by reducing or stopping work altogether, or moving to a different role, or perhaps taking up a new hobby.

We'll move to a new cash flow pattern, and possibly freak out a little at how much we're spending. We'll soon learn how to manage this though, and settle into a new rhythm pretty quickly.

We will change how we're using our surplus cash, moving away from an accumulation approach to what financial advisers call a decumulation approach, aiming for careful maintenance or managed erosion of capital over time.

In this section of the book we will cover the things to consider when setting up our retirement income and drawing from our assets. We'll address some dangers and how to avoid them and, importantly, I'll show the method I use to give your pensions and investments the best chance of lasting for as long as you need them to.

Phase 3: The New Normal

Pretty soon we'll have settled into a steady cadence of life in retirement. We'll have got used to how things work now and enjoy living in the present, making the most of our time, health and energy.

We will have a grasp on how our investments are holding up, and spending patterns will have settled down nicely.

We will be reviewing our finances annually or in light of any significant changes. But for the most part, things don't change very much so we don't have to spend too much time doing this, which is a good thing!

We can't help but think about the end game though. What if we lose a partner? What if we die first? What if one or both of us needs care? What if we can no longer make decisions for ourselves – who will look after us?

And finally, what will happen to our estates after we are gone? Can we make sure that our wishes are clear and that everyone's needs are met? What about inheritance tax (IHT) – can we make sure that as much as possible goes to our families or the causes we care about, rather than the government?

To a greater or lesser extent, all of us go through these phases and need to understand them so we're prepared to make the most of the opportunities they present.

In the many years that I have been presenting Meaningful Money, I have often said that if there's one time in life that *everyone* can benefit from getting professional advice, it's in the run-up to retirement. I stand by that comment while making it my goal to equip you as well as I can in this book to go it alone. If nothing else, you will be able to work collaboratively with an adviser, knowing the questions to ask and the mechanics of the process.

Phase 1

The Home Straight

THE FIRST OF OUR THREE phases of retirement is the Home Straight. Here's where we need to get everything organised and make sure we understand what we have, where it is and how it works. We need to dig out our paperwork and contact our pension and investment providers to fill any gaps.

We should understand how pensions and investments work generally, so that we can make sure that what we have got will serve our needs, or whether we should look to move money around.

This is where we make our plans and set out our stall for what we want our retirement to look like. It's where we get a sense of what the run-in to retirement has in store and whether we need to make some changes to make the most of our retirement funds.

The Home Straight is where we make sure we are ready. We have some work ahead of us, but don't worry, I'll guide you through what you need to do.

Let's get to it.

Chapter 4
Making Plans

EVERY JOURNEY SHOULD START WITH a destination in mind. If we know where we are now, and where we want to be, we can try to plot a course to get from here to there.

This chapter will help you understand why it's important to make plans, even though we know that sometimes life has other ideas! I'll give you some key questions to ask yourself about what's important to you, and we'll start to get a grip on our spending and how that reflects those priorities.

Everything you need to KNOW

Plans are nothing, but planning is everything

This heading is a quote from US President Dwight D. Eisenhower.

If anyone asks me what I do for a living, I will always say that I'm a financial planner. Partly I do this because most people don't know what a financial planner is or does, so it tends to spark interest. I also do this because if I say I'm a financial adviser, people often back away making the sign of the cross, thinking that I'll try to sell them an endowment policy or similar!

My job is about planning my clients' financial trajectories, and everything starts with goals and objectives.

Without a clear picture of what we want to achieve, there's no way our plans will come anywhere close. We may as well wear a blindfold and have someone spin us around 50 times before we set off.

I love to spend time with my clients getting to know what really drives them. Often, they have never sat down and done this for themselves, and I do understand why – we are all busy.

My clients frequently say that the process of taking the time to talk about goals and objectives is worth the fees alone, and that's especially true when we're dealing with a couple. It's amazing what has come out of these conversations that couples have never discussed between them before.

My expertise is to help clients articulate their dreams and then work with them to establish a set of practical steps they need to undertake to achieve those dreams.

The practical steps are the plan, but President Eisenhower was correct – that's nothing. It is the *process* of planning that carries the value. Shortly, I'll give you some prompts to help you discover what is truly important to you.

Plans are (at best) educated guesswork

We want to create a plan for retirement, but we should know from the start that our plan will be wrong.

Boxer Mike Tyson is famous for, among other things, this quote: "Everyone has a plan until they get punched in the face."

The point of Mr Tyson's comment is that planning is done in the abstract, whereas the thing we're planning for – our retirement, indeed our life – is very much a real-world thing. We can plan as much as we want, but the second our plan hits the real world with its myriad uncertainties, we know that our plan is going to be wrong.

Let me complete Mike Tyson's quote with the lesser-known second half: "Everyone has a plan until they get punched in the face. Then… they stop in fear and freeze."

If we start by understanding that our plans are going to be wrong and that before too long, something is going to come along that requires us to rethink things, then when that does inevitably happen, we won't be surprised. We shouldn't freeze in fear, but instead nod to ourselves, reassess things and move forward.

The process of planning prepares us for these surprises because we will have considered as many scenarios as we can in advance. When planning for clients, I always stress-test the plans and try to break them, so that we know what *really bad* looks like.

Inflation is a huge factor when we retire

Assuming we're 65 when we retire, then we should be planning for at least a 25-year retirement. Actually, the current average life expectancy of a 65-year-old male is 19.7 years and for a female it's 22 years. This is predicted to rise so that the average male who is 65 in 2045 should live another 21.9 years and a female another 24.1 years.[7]

Twenty-five years is a long time, right? A great deal can happen in that time, but one thing that will definitely happen is that your plans will be mercilessly affected by inflation.

When we're working, we don't think about inflation much. Writing this in early 2024, we're coming out of a period of the highest inflation figures for 40 years and things are returning somewhat to normal, whatever that means. But other than anomalous periods of time like we've seen recently, we don't hear or think too much about inflation because for the most part when we're working our earnings rise somewhat in line with it. We just don't feel its impact on our day-to-day lives.

This is very different in retirement when we don't really have the option to go for a better job to increase our earnings, and some of our income may be fixed at a level amount.

Over time, inflation *ravages* the buying power of our wealth.

Say you needed £30,000 a year to live on 25 years ago, in the year 2000. Now, thanks to inflation, that same lifestyle is costing you £55,500.[8]

If you retire at age 60, your lifestyle will end up costing you twice what it did at the start if you reach age 90, assuming a 3% inflation rate. Hopefully, you'll have some growth on your pensions and investments to be able to sustain your spending, but if not, you may have to make some adjustments and tighten your belt, or risk running out of money altogether.

I don't want to worry you, but we all need to understand just what a silent killer inflation is. I always hammer this point home with clients, and I will do here as well, as we go through the book.

My regulator, the Financial Conduct Authority, talks a lot about investment risk and volatility and all sorts of things pertaining to investment, but to my mind there's really only one real risk in retirement – that you will run out of money before you run out of life. Inflation is the biggest variable in this, and we are powerless to influence the world economy and central bank policy which affects it.

But we can manage our own spending and our investments and pensions in light of the inflation variable, and we must, to keep the silent killer at bay.

Chapter 4: Making Plans

Everything you need to DO

Sit down and dream

It's time to open a bottle of wine, turn off the phone and think about what you really want in life.

What would a great retirement look like?

I sometimes use the following three questions as a hook for doing this. They were first coined by the father of financial life planning, George Kinder.[9] My wife Joanne and I have discussed our answers to these questions as part of our own planning – they focus the mind and bring out some great answers.

Here they are.

1. Imagine that you are financially secure, that you have enough money to take care of your needs now and in the future. How would you live your life? Would you change anything? Let yourself go: don't hold back on your dreams. Describe a life that is complete, that is richly yours.

Note that this question doesn't say that money is no object, just that you have enough. Whenever I ask this question of clients, I find that their answers are still grounded in reality – they don't suddenly start talking about Bentleys and yachts and living in Monaco.

By removing the need to earn money to live, and removing the limitation of running out of money, the question encourages you to dream about the perfect life for you.

Use this question to tease out the things that you would love to do, the things you'd like to buy and how you would like to use your time.

2. Imagine that you visit the doctor who tells you that you only have between five and ten years left to live. You will remain as healthy as you are today and you won't feel sick, but your time is restricted. What will you do in the time you have left?

This question focuses the mind on how you would use your time if you knew it was finite. We all know this deep down, of course, but putting a time limit of five to ten years on things can really make us think.

In this situation, you would probably take the holiday you'd always wanted to take but didn't think you could really afford. If time is short, how do you make the most of it? This question doesn't assume infinite funds to blow in your remaining years – the answers still need to be grounded in reality. It is asking what you would do, in your situation, if you knew your time was short.

This question also forces us to consider what we may need to tidy up and put in order, so as to leave things in a good position for those who have to sort everything out after we've gone.

3. Finally, imagine that your doctor says you have 24 hours left to live. Notice what feelings arise as you confront your very real mortality. Ask yourself: What did I miss? Who did I not get to be? What did I not get to do?

Here, the idea is to help you think about your possible regrets. Where did you want to travel but kept putting it off? What did you want to say to someone, but never got the chance? What career or lifestyle choice did you decide against out of fear?

More than the things you never got to do, consider the person you didn't get to be. If you get the chance, read Bronnie Ware's powerful book *The Top Five Regrets of the Dying*. Death-bed regret is a terrible thing when we are powerless to change our life.

If you're in a couple, do this exercise separately but come together to discuss your answers. Give each other the space to talk and don't belittle or dismiss anything the other says. If you've been together a long time, you'll find there's a good deal of alignment anyway, but you may still be surprised at your partner's responses, so keep an open mind.

If you're flying solo, then write down your answers and revisit them over a few days. Let them simmer until you have a clear picture of what your ideal future might look like.

All this work should provide you with a kind of raison d'être for all the planning and sorting we're going to do.

Think about timescales

Having given some thought to what an ideal life might look like, we need to give some thought to when we might want to be living it!

While it is likely to be somewhat fluid, having a point in time when we'd like to achieve our goals gives us something to work towards. It also means we can work back from there to determine what we need to do now to ensure that we get there in the time we have left.

Don't necessarily choose arbitrary ages like 50, 60 or even the state pension age, which will be different depending on when you were born. Just because they're specific numbers doesn't make them special!

You could think in terms of years from now, perhaps. If you're a couple and want to retire together, that makes more sense if you're different ages.

It really doesn't matter when it is, just think about when you would like to make the Great Transition so you have something to work towards.

Look at your spending patterns

In Chapter 2 I reminded you that cash flow is everything. We'll get to the inflow part of that in the coming chapters, but for now you need to think about your spending.

You should be intimately familiar with what you are spending now. If not, then this is a high priority for you. You need to know what you're spending, in broad categories.

Consider three levels of necessity with your spending:

1. **Basic**. The things we need to live. Food, fuel, simple clothing, travel costs to work, basic insurance, mortgage or rent payments, internet access, etc.

2. **Leisure**. The things that make life a little more pleasant. Meals out, events, clubs and societies, expanded TV and streaming packages, hair and beauty treatments, one holiday a year, maybe.

3. **Luxury**. Non-essentials that we treat ourselves with. Spa days, a second (or third!) holiday, upgrading the car, flying business class.

Some of these costs, like commuting or parking charges, will stop if you give up working. Retiring may have an impact on your wardrobe and grooming costs too.

Ideally, you will have paid off your mortgage, if you own a house. If you still have a mortgage now, make paying this off part of your plans. Nothing brings peace of mind like knowing that no one can kick you out of your home.

When you know what you are spending now, you should be able to build a picture of what an ideal spending pattern in retirement might look like. You want to make sure you have enough money to meet your basic expenses, but there's no fun in just that. Ideally your retirement provision should cover leisure costs and maybe some luxuries too. This latter category needs to be the things that you would be prepared to give up. If things get tough in retirement or before, this is where you would tighten your belt first.

We want to get to a point where we can picture what life would look like, what it would cost each month or each year, and when we'd like to be living that life in earnest. Something like:

> We would like to have a lifestyle of £3,000 per month, which would allow us to take one holiday to Europe each year, change the car every five years and maintain our charitable giving. Of this, £2,000 per month is our basic requirement. We would like to achieve this ten years from now.

With the goal laid out, we now need to take a good hard look at our current situation – the starting point of our journey.

Chapter 5
Taking Stock

WE NEED TO SHIFT BACK to the other end of our journey. We've spent some time looking at the end goal, now we need to have a detailed view of where we are right now – our starting point.

Many of us don't keep enough of an eye on our finances throughout life, so we end up having a tenuous grasp on our financial situation at best. We're not totally sure how much we have, or how it's invested, or what it might all add up to. It's time to fix this so we know what we're working with.

You may have several pension plans if you have worked for different employers during your working life. Do you know who the plans are with, how much they may pay out on retirement and whether they have any additional benefits attached to them?

In this chapter we will concentrate on gathering together all of our financial information – that is all of our investments, pension policies, investments and bank accounts.

Everything you need to KNOW

Most people are bad at this

I think it is important not to beat ourselves up too much if we have let our finances drift. In my experience this is the normal state of affairs; most people don't pay enough attention to their money.

After all, we're not taught the basic financial disciplines in school or college, so we have either had to work it out for ourselves, or perhaps we were lucky to have a good financial role model in our parents or someone else.

There are also many distractions and other valid ways to spend our time than tidying our financial houses! So don't berate yourself or waste time on regrets. What's done is done, and we're moving forward now.

Disorganised finances lead to bad outcomes

This might sound like an obvious point, but it's worth saying. If your finances are chaotic, the chances of something going wrong are increased.

For one thing, all financial decisions are best made with a clear view of your current situation. If you don't have that, then you're likely to miss something important.

I had a client come to me who didn't really know how his pension was invested. He had no intention of taking benefits from the plan, but it was approaching the original retirement he had set decades earlier and had been 'lifestyled'. This means that the fund had increasingly moved into 'safer' assets like bonds. We were now in 2022 and his fund had reduced in value by a quarter due to the new investment mix. Had he had a better eye on things, he could have headed off this problem.

In this case it wasn't a bad decision, but rather neglect that was the problem. It was an error by omission, but it could have been avoided.

Simple is best

I have seen all kinds of financial arrangements in my time as an adviser, but one all-too-common mistake is treating complexity as a badge of honour. Usually, complexity is arrived at by default and neglect. People end up with nine pension pots because they haven't bothered to tidy them up throughout their lives. It's not as if they have intentionally chosen to set up so many different plans.

When it comes to organisation of your financial plans, simple is best for a couple of big reasons:

> Simplicity leads to better engagement on your part. You're more likely to get stuck into optimising your finances if you don't have an unholy mess to untangle first. If everything is orderly then you can dip in and out when something needs sorting, and the very thought of it won't fill you with dread.

> Simplicity also keeps costs down. If you have pensions plans from years ago, for example, there's a good chance that the charging structure is archaic and expensive. You could be throwing money away by neglecting these pots. It may also be the case that you are paying too much tax, which nobody wants.

Let's look at how to collect everything together and get a thorough grasp on where you are.

Everything you need to DO

Gather everything together

Wherever you have financial papers, take them out and bring them together in one place. Clear space on your dining table and put everything into one big pile. If you're already somewhat organised, then make piles according to your system – you can probably avoid some of these steps.

If you're the kind of person who 'files' things in their email inbox, this is going to be a bit trickier, but still not an insurmountable task. Use the search function in your inbox to look for any information about any pension policies and investments you know are in there. Print off the most recent information you have.

If you have online accounts of any description, consider printing off an up-to-date statement for each from the website. I know that paper is old school and not great for the environment, but I think there's value in seeing and holding tangible proof of everything you have.

Make a first pass – sort by policy

First, you want to go through every single piece of paper and group them together by type. By 'type' I mean any financial arrangement. So it includes your workplace pensions, personal pensions, investments, life insurance, savings accounts, National Savings – everything.

Check the policy numbers and account numbers because while financial institutions change their name more often than I change my socks, it's rare for a policy or account number to change.

Second pass – put in date order

Next, go through each pile you have made and sort things into date order, with the newest documents at the top. Don't throw anything away just yet, even if it is 30 years old – we'll get to that.

Create an index

Take a notebook, or a spreadsheet if you're that way inclined, and make a simple list of each financial arrangement you have. Doesn't matter about the order yet, just the provider, the policy or account number, the type of policy or investment, who it is with and maybe the current value.

Have a column with a checkbox to show whether you have up-to-date information. With many financial arrangements you'll only get a statement once a year, and sometimes these arrive a couple of months after the date they refer to. If the latest piece of paper is, say, 15 months old or more, then you're going to need to contact the provider(s) for up-to-date information.

Think back to fill any gaps

It may be that you have no record of some financial arrangements at all. Wasn't there a pension scheme at that company you worked for 17 years ago? Whatever happened to that? Didn't you have some Premium Bonds at one time? Do you have the certificates?

If there's an obvious gap that you don't have any information about, note that down in the index with a question mark next to it. You're going to have to do some digging.

Fill the gaps

Get the latest information

If you have financial information but it is more than 15 months old, then call the provider using the number that is always on the paperwork and ask for an up-to-date statement. Check that the provider has your current address and that your name, date of birth and national insurance (NI) number are correct at their end. Might as well sort these things out now to save some grief later on.

Keep track of your requests and make a note of turnaround times. If Company A promises you an update in five working days, mark your calendar and if they don't deliver, get back on the phone to them.

Find lost pension policies

If there are investments that you are convinced should be in your paperwork but are mysteriously absent, you're going need to do some detective work. Usually this applies to pensions from old employments. I recently had a client who had lost track of an old workplace pension that ended up paying him £25,000 a year! But do you also know who your long-term bank deposit is with – the one you took out more than three years ago?

The best place to start with old pensions is the Money Helper website, and specifically this page: meaningfulmoney.tv/pensiontracing (that's a shortened URL to make it easier to type in – the full address is in the footnote).[10]

There are some draft letter templates there as well as links to the pension tracing service itself which can help you track down old plans.

Again, be armed with your date of birth and NI number when you end up calling or writing to these companies. These don't change, unlike your address, so they will be needed to track down your pension plans.

If you know the name of your employer when you worked there, it will help, even if they have subsequently changed their name or gone out of business.

Tidy your filing

Given that you now have tidy piles on your dining table, it makes sense to get them into a system which will make it easier to find information in the future.

My preferred method of financial filing is in a filing cabinet, with hanging files, all neatly labelled.

If you don't have the amount of paper that would justify the space and expense of a filing cabinet, then you can get filing boxes which serve much the same purpose. You want a section for each policy or account ideally, with the most recent document at the front, where it's easy to see and reach.

If you feel like you have a *lot* of paper, I would still caution against throwing too much away until you really have a handle on everything. You could keep, say, the last three years of information on hand, and archive the rest in a box in the loft. You know it's there if you need it, but it doesn't clutter up your day-to-day system.

If you have the original policy documents, definitely keep these handy. Plenty of people lose them, and it's not the end of the world if you have, but they may be needed if you end up claiming on a policy or transferring it to another provider.

You can throw away any generic information, like the covering letter or shiny 'Update from the Chairman' leaflet that comes with your statement. Keep anything which is specific to your policy or account, and chuck away anything that is just filler. Make sure you shred anything with an address or other identifiable information on it.

Just promise me this – don't ever 'file' documents in the envelopes they came in. Envelopes are the work of the devil. They make it so much more difficult to find what you need and bulk up your filing space unnecessarily.

With your paperwork in order and all gaps in your financial history filled, you can start to understand what you have and what it might all amount to. In the next few chapters, we're going to discuss the main components of a portfolio so that you can make sense of the jargon on your documents.

Chapter 6
The UK State Pension

THE UK STATE PENSION HAS been around for over a century, tracing its roots back to the Old Age Pensions Act of 1908. Since then it has been expanded and developed, culminating in a much simpler state pension for anyone claiming it after April 2016.

For most of us, it forms the backbone of our retirement income and we need to know what we're likely to receive and when.

Everything you need to KNOW

The old state pension

Prior to April 2016, the state pension was a two-tier system, made up of a basic state pension and an additional level of pension called the state second pension, or S2P. S2P replaced an earlier version which was called the State Earnings Related Pension Scheme, or SERPS.

It was complex with different components and eligibility criteria, which meant it was difficult for anyone to fully understand what their provision was and how they could improve it if needed.

Contracting out of SERPS or S2P

The additional state pension in its various forms was designed to allow for those who earned more, and hence paid more in NI contributions, to accrue a larger state pension. It was a kind of government-sanctioned savings scheme with guaranteed returns at the end of it.

But in 1978 the option to contract out of SERPS/S2P was introduced. The thinking was that you could redirect the additional NI contributions into a personal or company pension in the hope of achieving better returns than the guaranteed benefits had it been left in the government scheme.

Many occupational pensions – those provided by employers – were contracted out by default. I remember in my early days as an adviser, we could sell stand-alone plans to accept these contracted out payments, and they were called *appropriate personal pensions*.

I mention contracting out because even though we now enjoy a much simpler, flat-rate state pension regime, the amount you will receive in state pension may still be affected if you have previously contracted out. I'll come back to this shortly when we look at what you need to *do*.

The new state pension

From April 2016, a new state pension system was introduced which is mercifully much simpler to understand.

Eligibility is based on your NI contribution record. You need a minimum of ten years of contributions to receive any state pension at all, and you will receive the maximum pension if you have contributed for 35 full years.

The state pension age has moved in recent years to reflect the changing demographics of the population – we are living longer and that means the burden on the state pension system is higher.

At the time of publishing, the state pension age is 66, and that's the same for men and women. It is slated to rise to 67 between 2026 and 2028 and then again to age 68 between 2044 and 2046. These dates are subject to change, of course.

The amount of the state pension changes every tax year in April, and is usually announced a few months before in the Autumn Budget. You can check what the current full pension amount is on the gov.uk website.[11]

The annual rise is governed by the so-called *triple lock*, which ensures that the pension level will increase by the higher of:

> Inflation, as measured by the Consumer Price Index, or CPI figure, usually in September.

> Average earnings growth, the idea here being that pensioners will benefit from improvements in the economy and wage growth.

> 2.5%, that is, if the other two figures are lower than 2.5%, then this figure will apply.

The triple lock is a real political football. I've lost count of the times when it has been threatened with change or even removal altogether. But it serves a real purpose in protecting retirement incomes, so I hope it sticks around for the long run.

Everything you need to DO

Check your provision

It is vital for your retirement planning that you know how much state pension you're likely to get. The best way to do this is to head over to the gov.uk website.[12] Just Google 'check state pension' and you'll get there.

You'll need to register for an account, but that's a straightforward process. Once logged in, the site will tell you what you will get based on your record to date and, if you haven't yet reached state pension age, it'll tell you what you could be expected to receive if you continue to make NI contributions between now and then.

You can also drill down into your NI record, which makes for interesting reading. It lists each year and tells you whether you have a full year or not. If not, then the site will let you know if you can make up the shortfall in that year by making voluntary contributions.

Consider making up any missed years

I just checked my own record, and it says that I have 28 years of full contributions and five years where I didn't contribute enough, notably when I was at university. Now, I know I don't look it, but I am 49 years old, so I have 18 years to go before I reach state pension age.

I have 28 years already, and I need 35 years of contributions to get the full state pension. That means I need to make seven full years of contributions out of the next 18 years, so I'm very much on track to get the full pension.

If I was age 65 and was seven years short in my contribution record, then I wouldn't have time to make up the shortfall just by working and paying as I go. In that case I should have the option to make up the shortfall by paying a lump sum to HMRC.

If you work out the maths, it's undoubtedly a good idea to top up your NI contributions if you can.

As I write, the state pension is £11,502.40 per year and this will rise each year under the triple lock. You need 35 years of contributions to attain this maximum pension income figure. So we can deduce that one year of NI contributions gets us a state pension of:

$$£11,502.40 / 35 \text{ years} = £328.64 \text{ annual income}$$
$$\text{per year of NI contributions}$$

The gov.uk website tells me that I could make up one of my incomplete years by making a voluntary contribution of £824.20.

So a £824.20 one-off contribution gives me a rising annual income of £328.64 – that means I'll make my money back in under two-and-a-half years from when my state pension begins. That's an excellent deal by any measure.

The amount you have to pay may be more or less than this, as it depends on how full each incomplete year actually is.

I find that the telephone helpline provided on the gov.uk website is actually very helpful. The agents know their stuff and can generally set you right. So if there's anything on the website information that you don't understand, that's where you turn next.

Watch out for COPE

When you check your state pension forecast, you may see a figure called the Contracted Out Pension Equivalent, or COPE. This is an indication of what extra pension you would have got from the state pension if you hadn't contracted out of SERPS/S2P.

I wouldn't pay too much attention to this figure. It isn't taken off the state pension, and it isn't paid in addition to the figure on the website. We'll get to what your other pensions will actually produce in the next couple of chapters.

Chapter 7
How Defined Benefit Pensions Work

DEFINED BENEFIT (DB) PENSIONS, SOMETIMES called final salary schemes, remain the gold standard for pensions in the UK. Unfortunately, they are very much in decline and are now mostly the preserve of the public sector. But you may have such DB schemes from your past employment, so you need to understand how they work and what they may end up paying you one day.

Everything you need to KNOW

Final salary and CARE schemes

The main thing you need to know about DB schemes is, well, the clue is in the name. The *benefit* you will get from a DB pension is *defined* by the scheme itself. It is a function of:

⇨ the length of time you are a member of the scheme

⇨ your earnings while a member

⇨ the *accrual rate* of the scheme, often expressed as a fraction.

Let's take each of those points in turn.

The *length of your membership* is straightforward enough to understand. It's the time from when you joined the scheme, usually at the same time you started working for that employer, and when you left the scheme. Typically, you leave the scheme when you find another job, but sometimes a pension scheme will close and that will be your 'leaving' date.

When it comes to your *earnings*, the definition of this is specific to each scheme. We often hear DB schemes called final salary pensions, but this is only one kind of DB scheme. It refers to the fact that the pension benefits are sometimes defined as a function of the salary you had when you left the scheme – your final salary while a member. Other schemes will use the average of your last five years' salary, or the best three in the last ten years or similar.

Finally, the *accrual rate* is the multiplier applied to the other two factors to work out the benefits. It is often expressed as a fraction.

Here's an example.

I work 40 years for a company and my final salary is £60,000. The scheme accrual rate is 1/60th.

The formula is:

(Membership length ÷ accrual rate) × final salary = Pension benefit

In this case that is:

40/60 × £60,000 = £40,000 annual pension

These days, an alternative to final salary is becoming more popular where the benefits are based on your average earnings while a member of the scheme. These are called Career Average Revalued Earnings or CARE schemes.

If you think about it, chances are that your income starts low and rises throughout your membership of a pension scheme. Or maybe, towards the end of your career, you reduce your hours or take a lower-stress role with a reduced income.

CARE schemes factor all this in by accruing benefits on a year-by-year basis. Often, the accrual rate on a CARE scheme is expressed as a decimal rather than a fraction.

Again, this is best explained by an example.

In my first year as a member of a CARE scheme, I earn £25,000 and the accrual rate is 2.25%. Let's say I'm 30 years old and the scheme pension age is 67.

The amount of pension I have earned in that year is:

$$£25,000 \times 2.25/100 = £562.50$$

So, from the scheme pension age of 67 I will receive a pension of £562.50 per year until I die, based on what I earned in year 1 as a member.

That's all well and good, but my pension age is 37 years away. That £562.50 isn't going to buy me very much then, thanks to inflation.

Well, the good news is that your earned pension is *revalued* between the year that you have accrued it and the year in which it will begin to pay out. The scheme rules will allow for an increase each year based on some measure of inflation. The idea here is that your £562.50 will still buy you that much worth of food, fuel or whatever in 37 years' time when you start drawing your pension.

PCLS commutation

All DB schemes come with the facility to take a cash lump sum, which is tax free, when you start drawing the pension. This is called the Pension Commencement Lump Sum, or PCLS, but most people simply refer to it as *tax-free cash*. Some schemes allow for this lump sum to be paid automatically, and others give you the option to *commute* some of your pension income into a lump sum.

Again, there's usually a commutation rate that the scheme applies, for example a 1/12 rate, which would mean that for every £1,000 of annual pension you give up, you get a £12,000 lump sum. Note that there is a limit to how much you can commute into cash – your scheme will tell you what that limit is in your case.

We'll come to this in the Great Transition section of the book, but for now I want to sow the seed that sometimes it doesn't make sense to take the lump sum just because it is available. When something is described as tax-free cash, this seems like something that is worth snapping up – a no-brainer. But we don't do *anything* without engaging our brain when it comes to our retirement. It may be that the income is more valuable to us than any lump sum, tax free or not. But we'll get to that…

Additional voluntary contributions

Many DB pension members want to make greater provision for their retirement than the default savings required by the scheme. They can do so in a personal pension unconnected with the main scheme, but many companies provide the option to make additional voluntary contributions, or AVCs.

Sometimes this works by purchasing extra years in the scheme. More usually, the AVC scheme is simply a defined contribution (DC) pension where the benefits are based on how much is paid in and the investment returns you get on your money. We'll learn more about DC schemes in the next chapter.

Making extra savings into the AVC scheme linked to the main pension does mean that your payments can be organised through payroll quite easily.

There is another benefit that only applies to some AVC schemes. When you come to retirement, your scheme may factor in the value of the AVC when working out what benefits you are entitled to. In practice this often means that the tax-free cash element can be taken from the AVC pot, which leaves more of the income from the main scheme intact – a useful benefit.

Chapter 7: How Defined Benefit Pensions Work

Pension Protection Fund

There's a reason that DB schemes are considered the gold standard for pensions. All the risk is taken by the employer sponsoring the scheme. They promise to give you an income at some point in the future based on the factors we have discussed, and it's up to them to make sure that the money is available to honour their promises to you and all the other members of the scheme.

The scheme takes your payments and those made by the employer and invests that money. These schemes are worth many billions of pounds in some cases. At regular intervals an audit is taken of all the members, both current and deferred, and also those who have already retired. A very highly qualified and well-paid person called an actuary does some complex maths and works out how much money is needed in the scheme to honour all of its commitments.

If there isn't enough money in the scheme, it is said to be underfunded. If there is a surplus, it is said to be overfunded.

Sometimes, if the sponsoring company gets into financial difficulties or even goes under completely, the pension scheme can also be in trouble. In these circumstances there is a government safety net called the Pension Protection Fund, or PPF.

The PPF is funded by levies on pension schemes and also from money recovered from insolvent employers' assets.

The PPF will cover most but not all of the benefits that a member would have received from their pension scheme before it was wound up. If your scheme is in the PPF, you will need to speak to them about the benefits you are likely to expect when you retire.

As pensioners tend to live longer these days, the cost of providing pensions has increased significantly, and for many employers who sponsored DB schemes, it has become prohibitively expensive. There are very few private sector DB schemes which remain open for new members. Indeed, many schemes have closed to existing members, with the employers offering DC schemes instead.

Transfers

It may be possible to ask the trustees of your DB pension to provide a figure called a Cash Equivalent Transfer Value (CETV). This is a lump sum that the scheme will give you to buy out your pension benefits. Effectively they are saying: 'If we give you £x, our liability to you is finished and we no longer have to provide a future pension for you.'

How the CETV is calculated is based on many different factors and will differ from one scheme to the next. It is intended to be a capitalisation of the benefits that you have under the scheme.

That transfer value must be transferred directly into another pension, usually a DC personal pension or a SIPP (more on SIPPs in Chapter 8), but note that transferring DB pension benefits is a very touchy subject in the financial services world.

There have been far too many examples of people being ripped off by shady advisers who have convinced them to transfer out of their gold-plated DB benefits and invest the transfer value instead in some dodgy offshore investment scheme. I've seen steelworkers who worked for 35 years to build up a fantastic pension, but who then lost everything to these charlatans.

Because of this there are all kinds of protections and safeguards for anyone looking to transfer their DB benefits. If the CETV is larger than £30,000 then you can't transfer it without having received regulated financial advice from a pension transfer specialist. The scheme itself will likely make you jump through all kinds of hoops and sign lots of disclaimers before they agree to the transfer.

The starting position is always that you *shouldn't* transfer out, and you should leave your DB pension in place. Only if you have very compelling reasons should a transfer be considered at all, and then only after serious thought and with professional advice.

But why would you give up valuable guaranteed benefits under a DB pension scheme in return for a lump sum paid into a personal pension?

Well, when you retire as a member of a DB pension scheme you will receive a guaranteed income for life, rising by some measure of inflation. All you have to do is watch it roll in each month. When you die, there will probably be an income payable to your spouse or partner, usually at a lower level, for the rest of their lives, depending on the terms of the scheme.

But what if you don't have a spouse or partner? The scheme is providing that benefit, but you don't need it. It would be better for you if they paid you more, instead of providing a benefit you don't need, but that's rarely an option.

Also, the income from a DB scheme stops when the second of you or your spouse dies. If you don't enjoy long lives, then the benefits may not end up amounting to much, despite all those years of paying in.

Also, there's nothing for your kids to inherit. As we'll see in the next chapter, this is not the case for DC pensions, so some people consider transferring out of their DB pensions to secure death benefits for their families.

Everything you need to DO

Right, now we have all that information in our heads about DB pensions, what do we need to do with it?

Get full details on your own DB scheme

You should receive an annual statement from your pension scheme. If you don't, then chances are that they don't have your current postal address, or they have gone paperless and you didn't read the letter about registering for their online portal.

Find the details for the pension scheme and call them. Use the pension tracing service[13] if you're not sure of the details. Either give them your correct address or ask for details on how to get the documents online.

You want an up-to-date statement showing:

⇨ the total length of your membership

⇨ the accrual rate of the scheme

⇨ if it is a final salary arrangement, what is the basis of 'final salary'

⇨ the normal retirement age of the scheme

⇨ how deferred benefits are revalued between leaving the scheme and retirement age

⇨ how benefits might be reduced if you retire earlier than the normal retirement age

⇨ and crucially, what income can you expect from the scheme at the normal retirement age.

This last one is the most important for your planning, but read the wording carefully – does it show the pension in today's figures or is it a future value? You want it expressed as if you were retiring today – that's the most meaningful figure.

If you're still a member of the scheme, does this retirement income figure assume you keep paying in until you retire? In other words, is it based on an assumed length of membership in the scheme?

If you have more than one DB scheme from past employments, get this information for all the schemes you have.

Summarise your benefits

The beauty of a DB pension is that its future benefits are known. The statement(s) you have received will have everything on it/them that you need to know, but to save you having to look through it/them all again in future, you could put a cover sheet on the file for each DB pension which has:

⇨ the normal retirement age (when your pension will start)

⇨ how much it will pay to you

⇨ how much it will pay to your partner

⇨ how it will increase, both before it pays out and after.

You should end up with something like the following:

The XYZ Ltd Pension Scheme

Pays £9,620 per year in today's terms from my 65th birthday.

The pension will reduce by a third and pay to my husband if I die first.

The pension will increase by 3% per year or CPI, whichever is the lower, both in deferment and after it pays out.

You should update this summary every year when a new statement arrives. It doesn't take long and means that you'll have an at-a-glance snapshot of what that pension is going to be worth, and you'll need that for Chapter 10.

Chapter 8
How Defined Contribution Pensions Work

DEFINED CONTRIBUTION (DC) PENSIONS ARE sometimes called money purchase schemes. The only thing that is defined in this case is the contribution, that is, how much you're putting in. What you'll get at the far end when you come to retire is unknown.

Whereas DB schemes are sponsored and managed by employers, with a DC pension, *you* are very much in the driving seat. That may or may not be a good thing – we'll see!

Everything you need to KNOW

A DC pension is just an account

Many people tend to have this perception that pensions are complicated. Looking to the past, that was definitely true. DB schemes and historical legislation made for a complex landscape of different options. When I was studying for my adviser exams, the Advanced Pensions paper was the one we all feared!

But these days the principles of pensions are much more straightforward. You can think of a DC pension as simply another kind of account in which to store money for the future. All you need to do is put money in over time and invest it wisely with the goal of amassing as large a fund as possible. Only when you get to the Home Straight before retirement do you need to understand what it all amounts to.

Crystallisation of your pension

Now that we are standing on the threshold of retiring and taking money out of our pension, we need to understand the mechanisms for doing so.

First, you can only take money out of a pension after age 55 unless you are in serious ill health. This normal minimum pension age (NMPA) is rising to age 57 from 6 April 2028.

While money is growing in your pension account and while you are adding to it, this money is said to be *uncrystallised*. In order to take any money out of a pension, you have to *crystallise* it.

Figure 1 shows the kind of picture I draw for my clients to help them understand this.

Figure 1: Crystallised and uncrystallised money

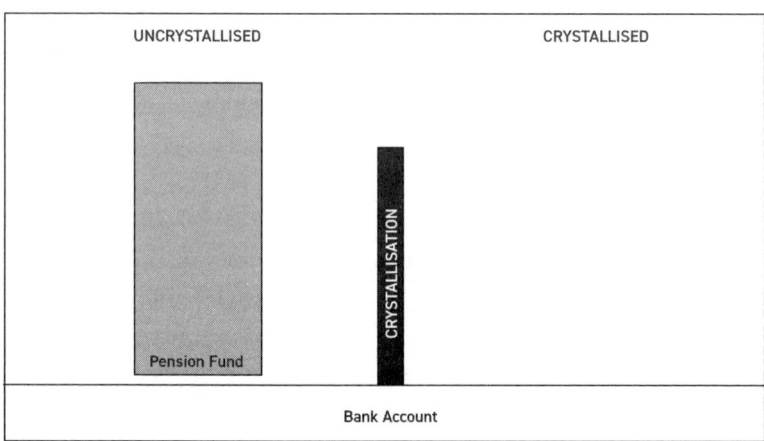

Chapter 8: How Defined Contribution Pensions Work

The figure is divided into three sections, one on the left, one on the right and one at the bottom. It's a bit like looking at a tennis net from the ball-boy or ball-girl's point of view.

On the left is money which is uncrystallised – for now, the whole pension fund is there. On the right is crystallised money, and I leave space at the bottom to represent your bank account, in other words, money that is available for you to spend.

So let's imagine you have a pension that is uncrystallised and you want to take your benefits out of it. This requires crystallising the fund and moving it over to the right-hand side of our diagram.

As the money moves across, you have the first of your choices to make – do you take your tax-free cash?

Up to 25% of your total pension fund can be taken as a tax-free Pension Commencement Lump Sum, or PCLS, as shown in Figure 2.

Figure 2: Taking your tax-free cash

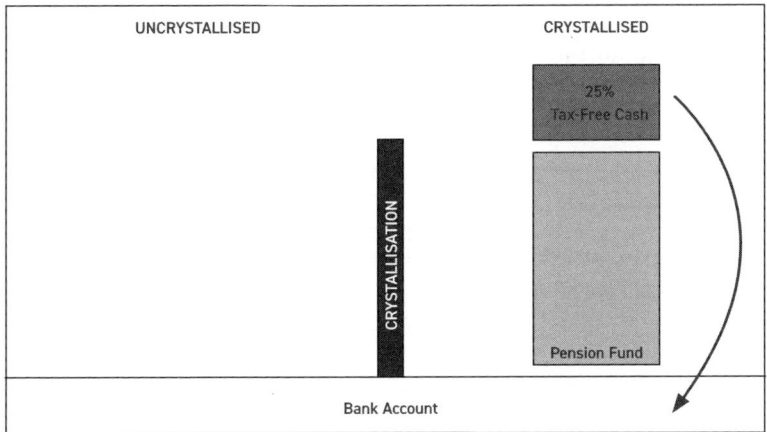

You don't have to take tax-free cash when you crystallise your pension fund, though the vast majority of people do so.

Everything that's left in your pension fund after you have taken your tax-free cash is now crystallised, and we have to decide what to do with it. Broadly, there are two options: flexi-access drawdown or an annuity. You can mix and match the two with different amounts; pensions are very flexible that way.

Understanding drawdown

Flexi-access drawdown (FAD), usually just called drawdown, has been around in some form since 1995.

As the name suggests, FAD allows flexible access to your pension fund. Before changes in legislation made in 2015, there was a cap placed on drawdown accounts limiting how much you could take out. The thinking behind that was to prevent people from completely spending down their pension funds and ending up entirely dependent on the state.

But now, you can take what you want out of your pension fund using FAD. You can take a regular income or ad hoc lump sums and you can start and stop withdrawals whenever you like.

If you have an old drawdown plan that was in place before 2015, you may still have the capped version, but it is easy to convert to FAD, usually in return for a small fee. Sometimes you will need to transfer your pension to a new provider if your current provider doesn't offer FAD.

Anything you draw from a drawdown account is taxable. In fact, it works much like PAYE when you're an employee – you will get payslips and a P60 at the end of the year.

That means, of course, that if you take a large amount out each year, you could end up paying higher rate or even additional rate income tax. To my mind, there's no sense in having a flexible pension and throwing a ton of money away in tax. Rather, we need to use the flexibility along with our understanding of the tax system to our advantage.

While the flexibility of drawdown is undeniably great, it can sometimes create its own problems. We may draw down too much and erode the fund altogether. Drawdown funds remain invested and that brings risk and the need to keep an eye on things. And sometimes we just need the reassurance of a regular income coming in.

Annuities

For those people who prefer certainty over flexibility, we can still call on a pension option that has been around for a very long time – the annuity.

At its simplest, an annuity is a guaranteed income for life. You hand over your accumulated pension fund to an insurance company, less any tax-free cash you might want to take out. The insurance company will pay you a guaranteed income for the rest of your life. Your capital has gone, but the income is a known quantity forever.

Of course, nothing in life, and certainly not in finance, is quite that simple. If you buy a *lifetime* annuity, you have options to choose from:

Spouse's benefit. You can provide for some or all of your income to be paid to your spouse or civil partner if you die first.

Indexation. You can have the income increase each year by a given measure of inflation. You will start with a lower income, but have the confidence that it will rise each year.

Guarantee period. You can set a minimum payment period for the annuity. So if you set a ten-year guarantee and you die after five years, the annuity will continue to pay to your estate for the balance of the five years.

Overlap. Here, your guarantee and spouse's benefit are paid simultaneously if you die. The full annuity will be paid to your estate for the balance of your guarantee period while your spouse also gets their benefit paid. Without overlap, the spouse would have to wait for the balance of the guarantee period before their pension kicked in.

Frequency of payment. You can decide whether your annuity is paid monthly, quarterly or annually, and you can decide whether you want it paid in advance or in arrears. If you opt for an annual annuity paid in arrears, you wouldn't get any money paid to you until the first anniversary of the annuity start date.

It is also possible to buy a *temporary annuity*, sometimes called a *fixed-term annuity*. Here, you set the income level you would like to receive and the length of time you would like to receive it for, say ten years. The insurance company will give you a figure for how much the annuity will cost to buy – the premium.

You hand over the premium to them and they'll pay you the income, just like with a lifetime annuity, the only difference being that the income will stop after the ten years are up.

You can sometimes build in a *maturity benefit* so that you get some of your premium back at the end. You may also be able to provide a *death benefit* if you die within the term.

As you can see, while annuities tend to be set in stone once you have arranged them, you do have some options on the way they are set up.

For a long time, annuities were out of favour. In the 15 years or so of low interest rates from 2007 to 2022, annuity rates were also low. That meant that the amount of income you would receive for every £1,000 of pension fund you gave to the insurance company was too low for many to consider. You had to have a big ol' pension fund to secure anything like a decent income.

Now that interest rates are normalising somewhat, annuity rates have likewise become more attractive. We are seeing a resurgence of people buying them to secure their income needs in retirement, but annuities are still nowhere near the levels from before the Great Financial Crisis in 2008–09. I think that we have been spoiled with the flexibility of drawdown for too long. I also have a nagging feeling that some financial advisers may be more likely to arrange a drawdown for a client because it usually means ongoing annual fees for them, while an annuity is a one-and-done type arrangement.

The last thing to say about annuities is that if you are in ill-health and your life expectancy is likely to be shorter as a result, then you will receive a higher income than you would if you had a clean bill of health. In the application, you would answer some detailed medical questions, and the annuity provider may write to your GP requesting some further information. They may then offer you an enhanced annuity for the rest of your life.

So then, we have flexi-access drawdown, on the one hand, and somewhat inflexible annuities, on the other. We have just a couple of other options to mention.

UFPLS

This might be my least favourite of all the financial services industry acronyms. Uncrystallised Funds Pension Lump Sum, or UFPLS, came about in 2015 with the pension freedoms, and is intended to extract a lump sum from your pension fund without going to the bother of setting up a drawdown plan.

Here's how it works:

You decide how much you want to take out of your uncrystallised pension fund, and the pension company pays it into your bank account (refer to Figure 3).

And that's it.

Whatever you take out is 25% tax free and the other 75% is taxed as income.

So let's say you want to take out a lump sum of £40,000 out of your pension fund. £10,000 of that would be tax free, and the other £30,000 would be taxed as income. If you're a basic rate taxpayer, you would pay £6,000 of income tax (20%) and receive a net amount of £24,000. Add that to the £10,000 tax-free cash and you have a lump sum landing in your bank account of £34,000.

Figure 3: How UFPLS works

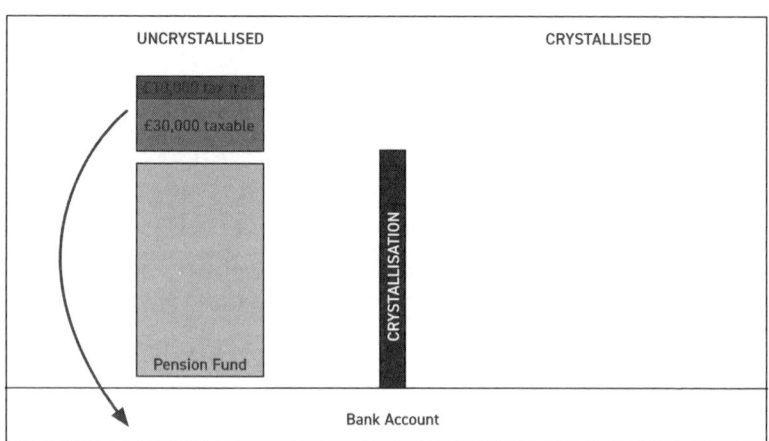

Here, no money ends up on the crystallised side; it doesn't even go there temporarily, just ends up in your account.

Why then, would you bother with FAD at all, when UFPLS is an option, especially as some pension providers even allow for monthly UFPLS payments?

The answer comes down to whether or not you need a large tax-free lump sum from your pension or can use it to make your income payments more tax efficient.

Let's say your pension fund is £400,000 and you need £100,000 to fund the purchase of your dream motorhome. In this case, you wouldn't opt for UFPLS because £75,000 of the UFPLS payment would be taxable. Instead you would probably crystallise the whole pension, take the £100,000 as tax-free cash, and leave the balance in a FAD plan to be drawn down when you need it in future.

New-style hybrid plans

The financial services world is pretty good at thinking up new options whenever there is a profit to be made. To that end, there

Chapter 8: How Defined Contribution Pensions Work

are a few different options starting to crop up which are neither drawdown nor annuity and aren't UFPLS either.

They are usually investment vehicles which sit on the crystallised side of the net and which offer the guaranteed income of an annuity, while still having a capital value. This means that you can switch back into a more ordinary stocks and shares type investment at any time.

These vehicles are usually a special kind of wrapper called a Trustee Investment Plan, and that means you can only hold them in a SIPP-type pension.

Ah, that reminds me…

Types of DC pension

Remember when I said that a DC pension is simply a form of investment account? That's definitely true, but there are some different types of DC plan you need to know about:

Personal pension. The most basic form of DC pension is a simple personal pension. They tend to be cheap and straightforward with few bells and whistles. Usually these hold investment funds. *Insured pensions* are a version of personal pension offered by insurance companies and you may also come across something called a *stakeholder pension* which is much the same thing.

Occupational pensions. These are DC plans that are set up by an employer. When you join the company, you are automatically enrolled into the pension and both you and your employer pay into it, unless you opt out. Usually the schemes are run by a third-party pension provider or insurance company. These are not to be confused with the DB schemes of the last chapter though. All the employer is doing is paying in – what happens at the end is up to you, not them. Payments are taken from you through the payroll system and get paid into the plan by your employer.

Group personal pension. This is just a collection of individual personal pensions grouped together to make it easy for an employer to manage, similar to an occupational pension.

Self-invested personal pension (SIPP). This is a kind of personal pension which gives you the option of investing in more esoteric investments like direct shares or commercial property, or the Trustee Investment Plans I mentioned just now. SIPPs can be more expensive than ordinary personal pensions due to this extra flexibility.

Essentially, though, these all work much the same way when it comes to taking money out in retirement. You will have to crystallise money, decide on whether to take tax-free cash, and then choose to buy an annuity, or go into drawdown or one of the other options.

Small pots

There is a special set of rules relating to small pension funds called the Small Pots rules. Small, in this case, refers to individual pension plans valued at less than £10,000 or if the value is less than £30,000 in total across all your pensions.

You can take the full value of any pension plan valued at less than £10,000 as a single lump sum. It's a bit like an UFPLS payment – 25% of it will be tax free and the rest will be taxed as income.

If your total pension provision amounts to less than £30,000 you can also take the lot as a so-called 'trivial commutation' taxed in the same way.

Taking small pots in this way also doesn't factor when it comes to calculating the pension lifetime allowance (usually shortened to LTA). These small pots are essentially ignored for any LTA figures, which may be of some use if your pension provision is very large.

We'll talk more about the LTA in Chapter 10.

Chapter 8: How Defined Contribution Pensions Work

Everything you need to DO

Well, that was quite a bit of information – turns out DC pensions are not so simple after all! So what's next, what actions do we need to take?

Find out what you have

These days, most of us have a few employers throughout our career, and that means that we often end up with several different pension pots here and there. Unless we have been careful to keep on top of them as we have gone along, chances are that we've lost track a bit of exactly what we have and where.

So it's time to dig out the most recent statement for each of your plans and gather some information, much as we did with the DB schemes. This time, the information we need is:

⇨ provider name and policy number

⇨ current value

⇨ what the underlying investments are

⇨ whether the pension offers FAD and UFPLS at retirement or whether you would need to transfer to another plan to access flexible benefits

⇨ whether there are any safeguarded benefits attached to the plan (see below)

⇨ costs for running the plan.

Safeguarded benefits (sometimes called safeguarded rights) are little added extras that sometimes feature in DC pensions, usually from plans from the 1980s and 1990s.

They are benefits like *enhanced tax-free cash* so you may be able to take more than the statutory 25% of the fund tax free. Or maybe a *guaranteed growth rate*, so the plan grows by a minimum of 4% a year, say, irrespective of what is going on in the markets. Some plans offer a *guaranteed annuity rate*, where the conversion factor of the fund into an annuity is written into the contract. Annuity rates were much higher when these plans came into being, and I've seen annuity rates of 10% and above in some cases. And finally some plans may offer a *guaranteed annuity*, which sounds like the same thing, but means the amount of income is set, not the annuity rate.

Again, your most recent statement should offer most of this information, but you should also approach each provider and request a retirement benefits pack from them. This should give you all the information you're going to need in Chapter 10.

If you feel you don't have information on all your pensions, then use the Pension Tracing Service to find out who to contact to get things up to date.

Summarise each plan

Again I suggest that you create a one-page summary for each plan, setting out the information I mentioned just now. I can't tell you how handy that is going to be as we go forward from here.

It will take a bit of work to decipher the information from the paperwork the pension provider sends you, but remember it is their job to help you if you need it. So if you're struggling, call them and ask to speak to them about it.

Be extra careful if you do come across any special safeguarded benefits – make sure these are highlighted on your summary sheet.

Weigh up the pros and cons

As we start to understand the different options available to us, our minds will inevitably start to think about which we might prefer. Perhaps you are drawn to the guarantee of annuities or prefer the flexibility of drawdown?

At this stage, let's consider the pros and cons of each.

Chapter 8: How Defined Contribution Pensions Work

Annuity

Pros	Cons
Guaranteed, stable income for life	Inflexible once set up
Flexibility in how the income is structured	Some or all of your pension fund is used up – you lose control of that money
Simple and easy to understand	Inflation risk – even though you can build in some protection against rising prices, there is a cost to this and prices may still rise quicker than your annuity
Protects against longevity risk – if you live a long time, it doesn't matter, as the annuity will pay	Limited facility to leave a legacy to the next generation
Facility to provide for spouse/partner	

Flexi-access drawdown

Pros	Cons
Flexibility and control over the invested pension fund	The fund remains invested and hence at some risk – you will need to manage the investments indefinitely
Ability to draw what you want from your pension – not limited by annuity rates	There is a risk that you may not be able to sustain your chosen level of withdrawals indefinitely – much depends on investment returns and the amount you want to draw
Any pension fund not spent can be passed on to your beneficiaries	Drawdown is more complex and requires reporting to HMRC etc.

Tax efficient – the fund continues to grow tax free and outside of your estate. Plus you can plan your withdrawals to maximise income tax efficiency.	No guarantees – all the risk for the longevity of your pension fund falls on you. Will you outlive your money or will your money outlive you?
Can still buy an annuity at a later date	

UFPLS

Pros	Cons
Flexible in terms of when and how much you can take from your pot	Taking large withdrawals could mean a large tax bill as 75% of the payment is taxable
No need to set up and manage a drawdown fund	Taking UFPLS triggers the money purchase annual allowance – a reduced figure for how much you can pay into a DC pension (currently £10,000 per year)
Tax efficient – 25% of whatever you take as UFPLS is tax free, with the rest taxed as income	No guarantees – much depends on how the uncrystallised fund is invested and how much you take out
Any pension fund not spent can be passed on to your beneficiaries	Not all providers offer UFPLS and even fewer offer monthly UFPLS payments

Each of these has its place. Having multiple tools at our disposal means that we can structure our finances very specifically for our needs, and we're going to get into that in Chapter 10.

Before then, we need to look at the non-pension aspects of our finances and see how they all fit into our picture.

Chapter 9
Everything That *Isn't* A Pension

WE'VE SPENT MUCH OF THE past few thousand words talking about pensions, and with good reason – pensions form the backbone of most people's financial provision in retirement.

But an ideal financial portfolio will also include ISAs, general investment accounts (GIAs), deposit accounts, Premium Bonds and maybe even some more esoteric stuff like VCTs, EISs and investment bonds.

We need to go over how these all work and where they too might fit into our plans for making the transition from saving and investing money, to spending it.

Everything you need to KNOW

How the different kinds of accounts work

Individual Savings Account – ISA

Other than a pension, an ISA is the one account that everyone should have. Its key advantage is that any money inside an ISA grows entirely free of all taxes and when you come to take money out, there's no tax to pay then, either. This is going to be useful to us in retirement.

There are five types of ISA, of which only four need concern us at the pre-retirement stage of our lives:

Cash ISA. This is simply a bank account in which any interest received is free of income tax.

Stocks and shares ISA. An investment account in which you can hold shares, bonds, funds and more besides. All income and capital gains are tax free.

Lifetime ISA. A special kind of ISA where you get a 25% bonus from the government on whatever you pay in, up to a maximum contribution of £4,000 per year. These are intended for those saving for their first house and if you take your money out for that reason, you get to keep the bonus and any growth on it. The same applies if you keep the money in the Lifetime ISA until age 60, at which point you can access it without penalty. If you take money out for any other reason than those two, you will pay 25% of the fund back to HMRC as a penalty. You can have a cash or stocks and shares Lifetime ISA. You have to be under 40 to open one and can only pay money in until you reach age 50.

Innovative finance ISA. Rather than cash or stocks and shares, these ISAs are designed to hold peer-to-peer (P2P) lending investments. These are high-risk investments whereby your money is lent to borrowers through an online platform. There have been some high-profile failures where investors have been left out of pocket, and unlike cash or stocks and shares investments, there is no protection under the government's Financial Service Compensation Scheme if your P2P platform fails.

The last type of ISA, the Junior ISA, is for children and so doesn't factor into our plans for retirement.

The annual limit that you can contribute to an ISA is £20,000 and this can be spread across all ISA types. As mentioned, the maximum you can pay into a Lifetime ISA is £4,000 a year, so if you max out that account, you have the balance of £16,000 to pay into a cash ISA, stocks and shares ISA or IF-ISA.

General investment account – GIA

This is a straightforward investment account with no tax breaks of any kind. You may sometimes see these named as a trading account, individual account or investment account. They usually hold stocks and share-type investments.

Any income produced by the investments inside a GIA is taxable at whatever your income tax rate is. This is true whether you actually receive the income into your bank account or not. When we are building wealth, most of us opt to reinvest the income to buy more of the investments we hold. But we would still pay income tax on that money.

Also, if we sell any investment inside a GIA for a profit, we may pay capital gains tax (CGT). More on how the two main taxes work a little bit later in this chapter.

Investment bond

These are less common than they used to be, but do still have their place for some investors. At its heart, an investment bond is a single-premium whole-of-life insurance policy. Let's unpack that:

Single premium simply means that you pay a one-off lump sum into an investment bond – it isn't something you could contribute to on a monthly basis.

Whole-of-life means that an investment bond doesn't have an end date; it is open-ended and can be surrendered at any time.

Life insurance policy – Wait. What? I thought we were talking about investing! The insurance element is usually 1% of whatever the value of the fund is. So, if you had £100,000 in an investment bond, if you died it would pay out £101,000. This nominal benefit means that the bond is taxed according to life insurance rules, and that has some advantages.

Life insurance companies and the investments they make suffer tax at company rates. This is deemed to satisfy basic rate income tax for investors, so if you are a higher or additional rate taxpayer, you're only paying basic rate tax on your investment as it grows inside the bond.

If you know you are likely to become a basic rate taxpayer in retirement, or maybe have some years where you earn no income at all, then you could use an investment bond to pay a lower tax rate when you are building wealth, and then no extra tax when you take money out later on.

When you take money out of a bond, a calculation is completed to work out if there has been a *chargeable event*. If so, then the amount of this gain produced by the event is added to your income in that year and if it takes you into the higher rate tax band, you will pay additional income tax.

There is never any CGT to pay on investment bond proceeds.

Investment bonds are issued by insurance companies and that limits the underlying investments you can choose to a range of funds offered by the company.

All bonds have the facility whereby you can withdraw 5% of the initial investment each year without any immediate tax implications. You can also defer these withdrawals, so if you don't take anything out for the first four years, you could take 25% of the fund out in year five with no tax issues. The amounts of withdrawals *are* factored into any future chargeable event calculations, though.

Finally, investment bonds can be held both onshore in the UK and offshore, often in jurisdictions like the Republic of Ireland, the Isle of Man or the Channel Islands. With these offshore bonds, the investments grow tax free. It's only when you take the money out later on that you'll pay any tax due, including basic rate income tax, which would have already been accounted for in an onshore version of the bond.

Enterprise Investment Scheme – EIS

An EIS is a tax-efficient vehicle designed by HMRC to encourage investment into the shares of start-up and early-stage companies. It isn't a wrapper or account, in the same way that a GIA or investment bond is. Instead it's a tax allowance that you claim from HMRC.

Investors into an EIS can claim up to 30% tax relief on investments up to £1m per tax year. This means that if you've paid, say, £12,000 in tax in any given year, if you invest £40,000 into an EIS you could get your tax bill wiped out. Note that you can't reduce your tax bill to less than zero. You have to keep the investments for at least three years or you will need to repay the tax relief to HMRC. You get twice the allowance – up to £2m per tax year – if you invest in so-called knowledge-intensive companies. I don't imagine many people reading this will be investing those kinds of figures!

You can use an EIS to defer CGT incurred from selling another investment. So for example, if you sold a rental property for a gain of £50,000, you could invest that gain in an EIS and defer the point at which you have to pay CGT on the property sale. You must invest in the EIS up to 12 months before and no more than three years after the other gain is made in order to defer it.

Any growth in the value of an EIS is tax free. Also, EIS-qualifying shares would qualify for business relief, which means they can be left to beneficiaries free of inheritance tax as long as you hold them for two years before your death. From April 2026, only the first £1 million of EIS shares would qualify for this exemption, with any value over that being subject to IHT at 20%. You can even offset losses made in an EIS against income tax using something called loss relief.

There are real tax advantages to investing in an EIS, but there's a very big 'but' to all this. As investors, *we should never, ever let the tax tail wag the investment dog.* That is, we should never invest in something that we don't understand or that we wouldn't ordinarily consider, just because the tax benefits are good.

EIS investments are high-risk by definition. Start-up and early-stage companies have a high failure rate. If you invest in a start-up and it fails, you will lose everything you invested. Of course, the reverse is also true – you may end up backing a unicorn (a new unlisted company valued at more than $1 million that is privately owned) and end up making a lot of money. Even if the company doesn't fail, you may find that the shares are difficult to sell, making it very challenging to realise your investment back into cash where you can spend it.

There is a very niche version of the EIS called a Seed EIS which only applies to very small companies where the income tax relief is up to 50% on the amount invested. If you have one of these already, chances are you have good tax advisers, so I won't go any deeper into these here.

Fact is, you shouldn't invest any money into an EIS or a Seed EIS unless you're prepared to lose it all.

Venture Capital Trust – VCT

There are some similarities between VCTs and EISs. Again, you can claim up to 30% tax relief, this time on investments up to £200,000 per tax year. You must keep the investments for five years to retain the tax relief.

Any gains you make are free of CGT and any dividends received from your VCT investments are also tax free.

The same caveats apply to VCTs that apply to EISs. The tax breaks are great, but the risks are high and you may struggle to sell your investments when you need them, so tread carefully.

Cash deposits

And then we have the myriad options for holding money on deposit. We have current accounts, easy-access savings accounts, notice accounts and fixed-term deposits. With all of these, which is best for you comes down to the interest rate offered and the accessibility of the money.

But be aware of the mantra echoed by financial planners: **Cash is *not* an investment.**

Say it with me.

Cash is *not* an investment.

What I mean by that is you don't build wealth by keeping money in the bank. In any normal situation, the interest you receive from money on deposit is lower than the rate of inflation, so that money is guaranteed to lose buying power.

You should only use deposits to hold money that you're going to use in the short term – the next one to three years, say.

I would include Premium Bonds in this, though they are a bit different. Here, you can invest up to £50,000 per person into Premium Bonds, and your bond numbers are entered into a monthly prize draw, where you can win prizes of between £25 and £1 million. Those prizes are tax free.

I actually really like Premium Bonds – they're a bit of fun, and unlike the Lotto, you get to keep your stake, though the chances of winning the big prizes are infinitesimally small.

Platforms

I want to address platforms in this chapter because they are a ubiquitous part of life for investors these days, and yet many people still struggle to understand their role.

A platform is simply an administration system, accessible by investors online and which offers a few different kinds of account under one roof. It's quite possible for you to open an ISA, a GIA and a pension on a platform.

Many platforms offer access to hundreds if not thousands of funds, to be held within the accounts. Other platforms, usually those run by fund houses, will only offer access to their own funds.

A platform takes care of reporting to HMRC if needed, reporting to the investor so that you have the info you need for your tax return and enabling you to see your investments online with one simple login.

I remember the days when if you wanted to buy a fund by Invesco, say, you had to fill in an Invesco application form and send off a cheque. Same if you wanted to invest in a Fidelity fund. Opening a GIA and an ISA with Jupiter would have required two separate paper forms.

A platform streamlines all this, meaning you have one place where you can hold different kinds of account and a rich portfolio of assets in one place.

Chances are that you have some investments held on a platform already. Which platform is best for you is partly subjective – you'll probably like the website or app offered by one platform better than another, for example.

But much comes down to the accounts and funds offered and perhaps most importantly, the cost. Some platforms charge a percentage of the money you hold there. Some will tier these percentages down if you hold more money there. Some will cap this to a pounds and pence figure, so you'll never pay more than £350 a year, say, no matter how much you hold there. And some will even offer fixed fees, like £10 per account per month, irrespective of the amounts held.

Property Investments

My good friend Andy Hart, host of the excellent Maven Money podcast, says the only assets you need to build wealth are 'businesses and bricks', that is, shares and property.

We have a bit of an obsession with property in the UK, and it's not hard to understand why.

Property is tangible in a way that stocks and shares are not. We can reach out and touch a property whereas our share investments are just numbers on a screen or a paper statement.

We have a sense that property will always be there and that, as such, its value can only rise. While that's not exactly true of course – there have been property price falls many times in history – like most real asset investments, given enough time, property prices do tend upwards as a general rule.

Many of us hold property as a pure investment, through buy-to-let houses or flats, or holiday lets. The building itself is a means to producing an income in rent, primarily. In return we as landlords maintain the property. There's a steady demand from tenants and holidaymakers, and new online platforms such as Airbnb make property-as-investment easier to do than ever.

A massive advantage of property is that its tangibility makes it an attractive prospect for leverage, that is, borrowing to invest.

If I buy a £250,000 house with a £200,000 mortgage and it increases in value to £350,000, then when I sell it, I have increased my £50,000 deposit to £150,000 with the proceeds of the sale. I could never have done this without the mortgage. I have only had to tie up £50k of my money, and I've used the bank's money to buy the property and benefit from its value increase.

Of course, I have paid interest to the bank, but chances are the rent I have received has covered that, at least in part.

Leverage can amplify both the returns, as in that example, or the losses. If the property I bought with a £200,000 mortgage developed huge structural problems or perhaps the place next door became a crack den, then the value of the property could indeed fall, perhaps even to less than I owed the bank. People may not want to rent it from me, so I wouldn't have the income coming in. I could end up being repossessed or having to sell the property at a loss, and even still owe the bank some money after the sale.

Property investing is very tax inefficient. You pay income tax on the rent, and over recent years the ability to offset mortgage interest against your rental income to reduce your tax bill has been made less attractive.

If you sell the property for a gain, you will pay CGT (more on that below).

You can't hold property in an ISA or any other tax wrapper. You can hold *commercial* property in a SIPP, but not residential property.

And there are massive duties and liabilities on you as a landlord. Legislation has made it harder than ever to evict your tenants and God forbid if anything happened to someone living in your rental and their injury or death was down to a defect in the property, you are on the hook for that and could be facing a prison term. There are myriad rules and regulations that you have to abide by.

Property is definitely not a panacea; it is far from the perfect investment. It has its place, if you have the stomach for some of the downsides I've mentioned, but is much more hassle than owning some shares in a fund on a platform.

That's why I've never invested in property directly, even though I've considered it many times. Really, I'm just too lazy to be a landlord!

Chapter 9: Everything That Isn't A Pension

Understanding the key taxes

I've alluded to the main taxes in my discussion of the various investment types above. Let me summarise how they work here so that you have a grounding before we start thinking about how to position all this for our retirement. Tax is, after all, a major factor in those decisions.

There are really only two taxes that concern us when it comes to taking money *out* of our accumulated accounts.

Income tax/national insurance

We don't pay NI on income received from our investments and pensions – so that's an easy one to put to bed. You generally only pay NI on earned income. That may be the case in some situations where renting out property is your main business or job, but dividend income from shares or interest from bank deposits is not subject to NI.

Income tax is charged in bands. The first band is called the *personal allowance*, and as I write, this is the first £12,570 of income you earn in any tax year. Income within the personal allowance is tax free. After that comes the basic rate income tax band, which covers the next £37,700 of income and is charged at 20%.

The next band is the higher rate band, which covers income between £50,270 and £125,140 – this is charged at 40%.

And finally, income above £125,140 is taxed at the additional rate, which is 45%.

Those rates apply to pension income, interest gained on deposits, rent from property, basically everything except dividends which are charged at 8.75%, 33.75% and 39.35% in each of the respective bands.

There are a couple of extra allowances. The *Starting Rate For Savings (SRS)* means the first £5,000 of interest earned is tax free as long as your other income is less than £17,750. If your other income is between £12,570 and £17,570, then the amount of tax-free interest you can earn reduces by £1 for each £1 your other income exceeds £12,570.

For example, if your other income totals £14,000, then that's over the £12,570 threshold by £1,430. That means that the SRS will only apply to the first £3,570 of interest earned:

$$£5,000 - £1,430 = £3,570$$

In addition to the SRS, the *Personal Savings Allowance (PSA)* provides for the first £1,000 of interest to be paid tax free if you're a non- or basic-rate taxpayer. If you're a higher rate taxpayer, the first £500 of interest is tax free, but if you're an additional rate taxpayer, you don't get a PSA.

It is possible to benefit from both the PSA and SRS.

Finally the *dividend allowance* allows for the first £500 of dividends to be received tax free no matter your tax status (2024/25 tax year).

These allowances are useful and we need to maximise our use of them if we can.

Capital gains tax

CGT is charged when you realise a gain on the sale of an asset.

There is an annual exempt allowance (AEA) which provides that the first £3,000 of gains (2024/25 tax year) made in a tax year are tax free. Everything above that figure is added to your income in the year, but only for the purpose of determining the rate of CGT you will pay.

Let's say you have made a gain of £8,000 this year. The first £3,000 of that gain is tax free under the AEA, so only £5,000 is taxable.

The £5,000 is added to your income, and let's say that it takes you into the higher rate tax band by exactly £2,500. This means that £2,500 of the gain would be taxed at the basic rate of 18%. The £2,500 that falls into the higher rate band would be taxed at 24%.

One important thing to mention is that there is no CGT to pay on gains arising from the sale of your main home, thanks to private residence relief.

Basic rules of tax

Confusing, isn't it?! While the rules, rates and allowances are real political footballs and can change at the whim of each successive chancellor, there are some high-level things we can take away from all this detail:

- We should use all the allowances available to us – pension tax-free cash and ISAs will be useful.
- Capital gains are taxed at lower rates than income.
- Property gains (excluding on your main home) are more highly taxed than gains from other assets, like shares.
- Dividend income is taxed at lower rates than other income.

These truths will help us when it comes to organising our finances optimally in retirement. Before we start positioning the pieces, let's look at what we need to do when it comes to the non-pension elements of our portfolio.

Everything you need to DO

Know your tax position in retirement

We need to try to work out what our tax position will be when we retire. This is complicated a little by the fact that we may have different sources of income being paid to us at different points.

Usually, by the time our state pension is paid, any other pensions we have will be in payment already, so let's take that as our starting point for now. We will get more granular when we discuss what I call the Danger Zone in Chapter 12.

Remember that we can only ever work in today's money, so we need to work out what our income would be if we were reaching state pension age today.

⇨ If you are due a full state pension, find out what that will be. That is the foundation of our income.

⇨ Next, if you have DB schemes, imagine you hit the normal retirement date today – what would the income payment be? We haven't yet decided on whether to take tax-free cash, so let's assume that you do for now. What will be the resulting income from the pension?

⇨ If you have property rented out, how much profit is it making for you after all your associated costs have been factored in?

⇨ If you have shares or funds paying dividends that are *not* held in an ISA, how much income is being received? Note that even if you're not actually receiving the income and instead are rolling it up into the investment, you're still deemed to have received it and will pay tax accordingly.

⇨ If you have large cash balances, how much interest are you receiving each year?

Add all this up and factor in what we know about tax allowances to work out our tax status. Here's an example:

State pension:	£11,500
DB pensions:	£17,000
Rent from property:	£7,800
Dividends:	£4,000 (first £500 is tax free, so only £3,500 taxable)
Interest:	£1,460 (first £1,000 is tax free, so only £460 taxable)
Total	£41,760
Taxable total:	**£40,260**

As this is well below the current higher-rate income tax threshold, we know we're going to be a basic rate taxpayer when all our retirement

Chapter 9: Everything That Isn't A Pension

incomes are in payment. We also know how much headroom we have before paying higher rate tax so we can factor this into our cash flow planning later on.

Get some details on your existing plans

Just as we have for our pensions, we need to understand the ins and outs of our current investments. We need to have them to hand for the purposes of planning what is best to do with them when it comes to funding our retirement lifestyle.

Here's a list of the information you need:

For all investments:

⇨ amount invested

⇨ current value

⇨ charges – ask for details of what you're paying at fund, account, platform and adviser level

⇨ breakdown of what funds you are invested in

⇨ details of penalties or charges for withdrawing money.

For general investment accounts:

⇨ a figure for unrealised capital gains – you want to know what the amount of gain would be if you sold the investment.

For investment bonds:

⇨ any previous withdrawals

⇨ a chargeable event calculation if you were to surrender the investment now.

As we have before, write a summary of this information for each investment you hold – we're going to need it in the very next chapter.

I feel like we've been building up to this for a while, but now – finally! – it's time to start positioning the pieces for a successful retirement.

Chapter 10
Positioning The Pieces

WE HAVE BY NOW SPENT quite a bit of time finding out what we already have in our portfolio of assets and sources of income. This is important because hardly anyone goes through their working life with a clear eye on the end goal. Most of us just do our best, sign up for pensions, put in as much as we can, shove the rest into ISAs and pick whatever funds we fancy as we go along.

Now it is time to start tidying things up and getting our portfolio in the best shape so that it can achieve two aims: *to enable us to live the life we want and to last the rest of our lives.*

That's what all the effort during our working life has been about, right? It's all for this – to give us a great life in retirement.

So let's look at putting things together in an optimal way.

Everything you need to KNOW

The three efficiencies

When considering how best to structure our portfolio for best effect, we're looking for three key efficiencies in everything we do. We want to make sure that the resulting portfolio is:

- ⇨ **Cost efficient.** We want to keep the costs we pay to providers, fund managers and financial advisers to a minimum, extracting value from every level of the chain.

- ⇨ **Tax efficient.** Every penny we give to HMRC is a penny we can't enjoy the use of ourselves. While it is our duty as citizens to pay tax, we should use every allowance and legitimate angle we can to reduce our tax burden.

- ⇨ **Hassle efficient.** No one wants to spend a moment longer than necessary managing a portfolio of investments and pensions. Retirement, however you define it, is meant to be a time of joy and fulfilment, and I reckon you can think of about a thousand things you'd rather spend your time doing than managing your money. So we need to make sure that whatever we set up needs as little ongoing maintenance as possible.

As with many things in life, there's a balance to strike. Here's an example.

In a bid to make things hassle efficient, we will consider consolidation of our various accounts. Fewer accounts mean less time in the management of them. But if we consolidate to such a degree that our portfolio ends up costing us more, then that's no good. We'll need to weigh up the cost of time spent in management versus the additional cost of the consolidation and find the right balance.

Chapter 10: Positioning The Pieces

Consolidation – pros and cons

Most of us have too many accounts. There's no judgement here. I see it all the time in my day job as a financial planner. We had someone come to us recently with 14 different pension plans, but I think the record might be the gentleman who died and whose son had to pick up the pieces to manage the considerable estate. There were 98 lines on a spreadsheet – 98 different accounts in four different countries!

We need to start from the understanding that less is more and that we need to get to the minimum number of accounts possible, without causing ourselves problems by doing so.

The benefits of consolidation are clear: less time in management, easier to maintain a consistent investment approach and probably lower costs as many platforms will offer lower charges at higher amounts.

In addition, consolidating onto one or two modern platforms may offer us a much wider choice of investments and some functionality that may not be available to us under old plans.

The main objection I get to any thought of consolidation is the old eggs in baskets argument – that more baskets means more security for our pension eggs. It is certainly true that you should never consolidate to the point of losing sleep over the perceived risk of your portfolio. I often leave client money invested on two or more platforms just to provide the reassurance that if one fails, they will still be able to get their hands on their other money while everything is sorted out. I go into a bit more detail on the protections for platform investors below.

To my mind, the benefits of consolidation outweigh the potential risk of having fewer provider baskets to hold your money in, but you need to decide this for yourself – how many providers is too few?

What if my provider fails?

I think it is worth considering the implications of the failure of one of our providers. Let's talk about investment platforms first.

Investment platforms

In the UK we have a set of rules called the CASS rules which mandate the clear separation of client money from the operating capital of the platform. The platforms have to reconcile their clients' trust account every day to the penny, so there's never any doubt about what cash belongs to which client. If the platform goes under, it can't take your money with it. Barring massive fraud, this is a very high level of protection.

The platforms themselves are subject to stringent capital adequacy requirements. That means they have to report to the regulator on the state of their finances. They also have to keep enough cash on hand to cover the cost of a liquidation in a worst-case scenario. Most platforms hold considerably more capital than the minimum requirement.

If a platform did go under and their clients lost money as a result, each individual investor would be covered up to £85,000 by the Financial Services Compensation Scheme (FSCS).

If you hold cash on a platform (as opposed to the money that is invested in funds) then that cash will be held with one or more banks. If those banks fail, you would be covered up to £85,000 for each bank that failed. You might want to ask your platform which banks they use in case you also bank with the same institution personally. You might struggle to get a straight answer though as some platforms will move money between banks fairly regularly.

Most of us will invest with one or more fund providers on a platform. The fund managers are themselves regulated by the Financial Conduct Authority (FCA) and are subject to many of the same capital adequacy rules as the platforms. If a fund manager failed and you lost money as a result, then you would be covered up to £85,000 per fund manager.

As you can see there's some complexity here. There's the risk of the platform, the bank where the platform keeps your cash and the underlying fund managers going under. Fortunately, this is very rare, and the FSCS has a history of being flexible and quick to act on the very few occasions a platform has gone under in the past.

Assuming you did have pensions or investments on a platform that failed, what would likely happen is that those assets would be bought up by another platform and reregistered there. You would receive a login from the new platform and life would go on. This might take a little while, and during that time you may have limited access to your money, but you certainly wouldn't lose any of your own money just because the platform failed. Once the dust had settled, you would want to look at the new platform and ensure its fitness for your purposes.

Even if nothing so drastic as a platform failure happened, there could be a serious outage meaning that access to the platform could be interrupted for a period of time, and that's reason enough to consider having at least two platforms for your money.

Sometimes we will have one partner's money with one platform and the other partner's money with a second platform. Alternatively, we may have a couple's SIPPs with one platform and their ISAs and GIAs with another. This can mean paying slightly more fees because the higher, combined amount could attract a lower rate of fees, but many clients see this as a price worth paying for the security of diversification.

I always encourage my clients not to lose too much sleep over this. The regulatory regime in the UK is extremely robust, and high-profile failures are mercifully few and far between.

Insurance companies

The rules are slightly different for insurance companies. Many of us have insured pensions – those provided by insurance companies. Often these are workplace schemes or just plans that we've had for ages, before everyone started getting SIPPs or platform pensions.

If you have an *investment* with an insurance company, like an investment bond, then the £85,000 FSCS limit applies if the provider fails.

But if you have a *pension* with them, then as long as it qualifies as a 'contract of long-term insurance' then you would normally be covered for 100% of any claim if the insurer failed, with no upper limit.

This sounds like a real benefit, but in practice, a long-standing insurance company is very unlikely to fail completely. Usually if a provider like this gets into trouble, it is bought by a rival pretty quickly. Also, insured pensions often have higher charges than a platform pension and a far more limited set of investment options.

Personally, I think the risks of failure are so small that we should not let our long-term investment decisions be driven by the fear of loss due to a provider collapse.

Retirement is not the time to reduce investment risk

Many people assume that as they approach retirement, they should reduce the risk of their portfolio. Their arguments sound logical on the surface:

> 'I'm going to be stopping working, so I won't have the income to keep topping up my portfolio if the value drops.'

> 'I have less time to wait for values to recover.'

> 'My pot will be finite and I don't want to return to work if the market crashes and the portfolio can't support me.'

While I would never dismiss those points, I think there's one fact that overrides them all – we need our money to outlive us, and we're likely to live for a long time.

Throughout our working life we have tended to see retirement as the end goal, and to an extent that's true, or certainly it used to be. Back when everyone bought an annuity with their pension fund, you would want to be reducing the risk of your portfolio as you approached that day – a 20% fall in the value of your pot in the six months before you bought your annuity could consign you to a 20% lower income for the rest of your life.

But now we have flexible pension options as we discussed in Chapter 8, so retirement is actually more like an inflexion point than an end point. The work we've done to amass wealth up to this point determines what kind of a life we're going to have in retirement.

But still, our retirement stretches out ahead of us. Most of us will be retired for at least a couple of decades. By any measure that's a long time that our money will be invested and working for us. We don't want to hamstring the portfolio by being too cautious with it.

I'm going to come to the main mechanism I use for managing risk in retirement in Chapter 15, but for now let's just agree that as our money is going to be invested for a long time, we need to be intelligent about the risk we take with it.

The pension lifetime allowance

As of 6 April 2024, the pension lifetime allowance (LTA) has been abolished, so you may wonder why I'm devoting this section to it.

The LTA was introduced as part of the badly named pension simplifications of 2006. It was intended to limit the benefits an individual can accrue into pensions without paying additional tax charges.

At various points in time known as benefit crystallisation events (BCEs), an individual's pension provision would be tested against the LTA at the time to see if a tax charge was due. There were 13 of these BCEs, but broadly they came down to just three main events:

⇨ taking benefits from a pension

⇨ reaching age 75

⇨ dying before age 75.

If you breached the LTA at any of the BCEs, you paid an additional tax of 25% of the excess, called a *lifetime allowance charge*.

I always hated the LTA as it seemed odd to me that the government should incentivise pension savings on the one hand with tax relief, and then limit things at the other end when people took their pension benefits. But tax reliefs do cost money, so I guess the LTA was a control on the extent of that cost.

One thing that is continuing is the limit on tax-free cash. This will be limited to £268,275, which is 25% of the LTA before it was abolished.

Some individuals with large pension pots or significant DB scheme provision may have applied for certificates which protect their LTA at higher levels. If you have one of these, you'll know, and in this case your tax-free cash is limited to 25% of your higher LTA.

As I write, much of the legislation for how lump sums will be tested and taxed is still being sorted out. Tread very carefully here and consider seeking professional advice if you have a pension provision which is likely to fall foul of these very complex rules.

Everything you need to DO

Consolidate

Having discussed the pros and cons of consolidating your various pots earlier, now is the time for you to start taking action in this regard.

As a baseline expectation, I would start with the assumption that you need just one pension fund and one ISA. There may be reasons why you can't or don't want to achieve this level of simplicity, but it's certainly something to aim for.

Let's start with your pensions.

Chapter 10: Positioning The Pieces

Pension consolidation

Remember that at a fundamental level, a pension is just an investment account. Obviously we're talking about DC schemes here. I'm going to work on the assumption that you draw your DB scheme benefits when they are due to be paid.

Pull out the information you gathered together in Chapter 8. Are there any plans with safeguarded benefits that should stay where they are? If so, let's just consider the straightforward plans for now – the goal is to pull these together into a single, flexible pension plan on a powerful investment platform.

Your first job is to choose a platform. Maybe you have one already that you love to use. Make sure any prospective platform ticks all the following boxes for retirement flexibility:

⇨ able to facilitate FAD and UFPLS

⇨ able to facilitate monthly tax-free cash payments and/or regular UFPLS payments

⇨ able to accept online instructions for ad hoc payments or changes to regular payments.

And then make sure that the charges are reasonable for the kind of investing you're going to do.

I believe that most people are best served with simple, long-term fund investing, but if you're keen to buy and sell stocks or funds on a regular basis, then you need to make sure that your chosen platform will make this easy for you, at a cost which is acceptable.

If you haven't already, open a pension account on your chosen platform. You will be given the option to transfer other pensions into this new plan. Enter the provider name and policy number of your existing pensions into the platform and they will then approach your other providers and ask for the money to be transferred directly.

You have two broad options for how this could work:

In-specie transfers. This is where the funds you hold in your old pensions are not sold, but simply transferred as-is to the new pension. This won't be possible if your old pensions are insurance company plans, but if you're moving from one platform to another, it might be. The advantage here is that you are not out of the market while the money is being moved around.

Cash transfers. Here, the funds are sold down by your old pension providers and the cash is moved to the new pension. While the money is in transit, you will not be invested in the market, so if it goes up you'll miss out, but conversely if it falls, you'll miss that too! Once the money lands with your new provider, you will need to place investment instructions to get it back into the market.

Generally speaking, a cash transfer will happen *much* more quickly than an in-specie transfer as it is a much less complex operation. A pension transfer can take anything from a few days to a few weeks, but it should never take more than six weeks. Make sure that you keep chasing things up to keep them moving in the right direction.

The financial services companies still aren't very good at talking to each other effectively, so it might be down to you to make sure your case gets actioned quickly. We spend a lot of time doing this chasing at my financial planning practice. My team knows the phone hold music for about two dozen different providers and can tell you which provider it is after just a couple of seconds. It's like the world's worst game of Name That Tune.

When all the money has landed in your new pension, it needs to be invested. We're going to go into that in detail in Chapters 14 and 15.

Pensions that can't be moved

If you have any pensions that should really be left where they are, perhaps because of some in-built guarantees, then all you need to do is note when you will be taking the benefits from them. Chances are the flexible benefits aren't an option here, so you will need to weigh up this restriction against the enhanced benefits.

If the pension has a guaranteed annuity amount or rate, then make a note of what this is likely to mean in terms of your income at the usual retirement age. Taking such a pension early will likely reduce what will be paid to you, so be aware of this too.

If the extra benefit is enhanced tax-free cash, then you will need to decide what to do with the balance of the fund when the cash is paid out. Usually the remaining fund can be transferred to your new platform pension, but only *after* it is crystallised.

Investments

Transferring investments works much the same way, including the in-specie or cash options. To transfer in-specie, the exact same fund would need to be available on both platforms. This comes down to the share class level, too.

Sometimes you will see different classes of shares offered by funds. Perhaps the investment manager has a deal with Platform A to give their users slightly cheaper costs for the fund than users of Platform B. This is usually achieved by creating a different share class which is only offered to Platform A customers. These are usually designated by letters, so you may see the XYZ UK Smaller Companies Fund C Acc. The letter 'C' here is the share class designation.

If you hold the fund on your existing platform but hold the 'D' share class instead, it's likely that your new platform won't accept the transfer in, so you will need to opt for a cash transfer instead.

It's very important to transfer your ISAs from one platform to the other so as not to lose the ISA wrapper. If you sell the funds, draw the money out into your bank account and then try to add it to an ISA on your new platform, you'll only be able to add £20,000 per tax year.

If you have a general investment account, it's usually the best option to transfer any funds across in-specie, particularly if you have made gains in your funds. If you sell down the funds and move the money in cash, you will incur a potentially taxable capital gain, so be careful.

Maximise pensions

Many of us will be at the peak of our earning power in the last years before we retire. Also, there's a good chance that you have paid off your mortgage, so your disposable income is possibly the highest it has ever been.

This is a great opportunity to make the most of the tax relief on pension contributions. If you are employed, consider salary sacrifice to make this as easy as possible, all done through your payslip.

If you have large cash balances, consider how much of this you could add to pensions while you still have the earnings to justify the contributions.

Remember that you can contribute up to 100% of your earnings or £60,000, whichever is lower, and get tax relief on your pension. And you can even contribute £3,600 gross into a pension if you have no earnings at all. If one partner is a non-taxpayer – let's say they are earning £10,000 a year – then they could contribute £10,000 into a pension, but it would only cost them £8,000. The extra £2,000 is tax relief, even though they're not paying tax. That's free money from HMRC – a real opportunity.

Hold some cash

You'll see in Chapter 15 that I have a method for investing in retirement that helps maximise the longevity of a portfolio by minimising the chance of having to sell assets if they are distressed.

A core part of that approach is keeping enough money in cash to spend in the near term, by which I mean the next couple of years.

In addition to this, I think it is wise to hold a buffer fund in accessible cash in an easy-access account. This could be a cash ISA, but usually just an online saver account will do.

You could be thinking about where that money might be now, and how to ring-fence it for this purpose. As we build our cash flow ladder in Chapter 15, we will make sure that this cash is spread between the accounts from which we need to draw. For now though, just make sure you have a good buffer fund behind you so that not everything is invested. This will give us the financial space to make changes to your investment approach later on.

Seek advice

This might seem an odd suggestion, given that this book is about helping you to navigate your own way into retirement without help.

On the other hand, it may seem a bit self-serving, given that I am a financial adviser!

On the Meaningful Money Podcast and in my videos, I've always been clear that if there's one time in life that anyone can benefit from seeking professional financial planning advice, it's when they're on the cusp of retirement. This is the point of peak complexity in most people's financial lives, and making the leap from accumulation to decumulation is one of the biggest decisions we'll ever make. Having a professional cast their eye over your plans can bring real peace of mind in that moment.

Let me give you some guidance on how to find a decent financial planner.

Notice that I didn't say financial adviser, but *planner*. There *is* a difference, and it's an important one.

Classically, financial advice was about selling financial products. You would meet with an adviser who would talk to you long enough to identify any gaps in your financial provisions that they could fill with a product. The adviser got commission, the client generally went away in better financial shape, and all was well.

Of course, commission-based selling was a recipe for conflicts of interest and so there have been many products mis-sold over the decades.

Fortunately, commission was abolished on investment and pension business in 2013. Since then, advisers have had to agree fees directly with their clients. Couple this with the rise of the internet, and it's clear that many clients are not happy to pay advisers for something they can do very well themselves in a few minutes online.

The best advisers have come to realise that what clients really value isn't the sale and administration of financial products, it's the two things they get from a financial planner: a process and a relationship.

The process goes something like this:

1. Establish a detailed picture of the client's current financial situation.
2. Help the client to visualise and articulate the kind of life they're hoping to build, and all their hopes and fears for their future.
3. Set the ideal outcome as the destination of the journey.
4. Use intelligent assumptions to project forward their current situation and see if they will reach their destination.
5. Identify and recommend solutions if they're not going to hit their target and other optimisations such as the three efficiencies.
6. Repeat forever.

The relationship is summarised in step 6, and should be strong and deep. I know things about my clients that their own family don't know and certainly their accountant, lawyer or priest don't know. A financial planner acts as a kind of financial GP, having a detailed overview of all parts of a client's life and financial situation, and calling in specialists where necessary.

At my firm we have a couple of client families for whom we are acting for the fourth generation. The relationship is over 40 years long in some cases. This would not be the case if we were just flogging products.

Chapter 10: Positioning The Pieces

At the same time, we are quite happy to take a one-off detailed look at someone's current situation and plans and give them the mechanics of what they need to do to move things forward. Essentially we're completing steps 1–5 in the list above. Then we wave the clients off and they take it from here. We think we can deliver better outcomes over a longer relationship, but we're happy to work this way if that's what the client prefers.

So how do you find a financial planner to work with, should you feel the need?

Start with personal recommendations. Have any of your friends or family worked with a good planner that they can recommend? As far as you know, are they in a similar financial situation to you? If so, then a recommendation is a great way to start.

There are search engines that specialise in finding an adviser near to you. Unbiased.co.uk and vouchedfor.co.uk are the biggest of these. They can help you narrow down a list to your local area and there are other filters you can apply too. Be aware though that some advisers will be paying more to show up higher in the listings, so this isn't an unvarnished list.

Look for individuals that are either Chartered Financial Planners, usually designated by APFS or FPFS after their name, or Certified Financial Planners who will have the designation of CFP.

At the company level, look for Chartered Financial Planners or Accredited Financial Planning firms. In each of these cases, the advisers and the firms they represent will have achieved a higher level of qualification than the average Joe. Of course, more exams does not necessarily make for a superior adviser, but to achieve this level of qualification does take time and commitment to the cause, so they're unlikely to be fly-by-nights who are just in it for a quick buck.

Any potential planner you see will have an initial conversation with you at no cost and without obligation. Think of it as a kind of courtship, where you can get to know each other a bit and see if you want to take things further.

Ask some key questions, like:

⇨ Are you willing to advise me even if I end up implementing any recommendations myself?

⇨ What are your charges and how do they work?

⇨ How would a long-term relationship work and what would it cost?

⇨ How will we contact each other – by phone, email, WhatsApp or maybe an online portal?

⇨ Do you deliver cash flow modelling?[14]

⇨ What are the timescales?

⇨ What level of wealth and complexity are you used to dealing with?

If a prospective adviser mentions their 'solutions' in that first meeting, like investment approaches or platforms, make your excuses and leave. That first meeting should be all about you, not them. It would be like driving into a garage to get work done on your car and having the mechanic give you a guided tour of their toolbox. The tools are irrelevant – it's the outcome you want the mechanic/adviser to focus on.

How can they help? Do they seem excited to work with you? The best advisers are zealots. We love what we do and where we see we can add value and help a client, so we tend to get a bit excited!

Whether you work with an adviser or not, you want to get your finances to the stage where:

⇨ You have the fewest accounts of each type and are happy with the level of consolidation you have achieved.

⇨ You have some cash on hand as a buffer fund, ready to spend as required.

⇨ You know when your guaranteed sources of income, like DB pensions and the state pension, will pay out, and how much.

⇨ You have a healthy balance between the types of account such as pensions, ISAs and possibly GIAs too.[15]

⇨ You have maximised your pension provision.

⇨ You have considered whether you can or should address the balance of assets between partners, where possible.

We're going to get to the investment approach *within* your tax wrappers in the next section, The Great Transition, but before we get there, there's an important subject we need to address.

Chapter 11
Catching Up

IT'S A FACT OF LIFE that not all of us reach retirement with sufficient provision to provide for a comfortable lifestyle.

If that's due to poor decisions made earlier in life, then we have to accept the consequences of those decisions.

For many of us though, there are some good reasons why we are where we are. I want to look at those and suggest some ways of catching up, because it's never too late to make a difference to your retirement provision.

Everything you need to KNOW

Women have it tough

A government report into the gender pensions gap in early 2024[16] shows some pretty stark differences:

⇨ Women retire with an average pension fund of £67,000 compared with the average men's pension pot of £205,000.

- ⇨ Childcare and other factors result in an average career gap of ten years for women.
- ⇨ This contributes to about £39,000 of lost pension savings.
- ⇨ The average wage for women is still about 25% less than the average wage for men.
- ⇨ In 2023 74% of women were in employment, compared with 83% of men.

Those are some pretty significant headwinds. We all understand the greater likelihood for women than men to take a career break to have and raise children. But there's pressure from the other end of the family age spectrum too, as women are often expected to care for ageing parents – the so-called 'good daughter syndrome'.

An average pension fund size less than a third that of their male counterparts is a huge challenge to overcome while simultaneously earning less – we'll look at what can be done about that shortly.

I'm sure the government would argue that they are making strides to address this, but it seems to me like things are being 'considered' but not a lot of action is being taken.

There are proposals to reduce the earnings threshold for auto-enrolment into workplace pensions and certainly there is more money available for childcare than ever before.

But I'm afraid it's up to us to address the gender gap in retirement provision – no one else is going to do it for us.

Divorce is a major financial risk

Many people get divorced each year and so need financial advice to establish their new starting position and what they need to do to be ready for retirement. There has also been an increase in the rates of divorce in older folks. In fact, the number of people aged over 60 getting divorced each year has doubled since 1993.

The assets (and debts) of a couple tend to be shared out on divorce and this obviously has a big impact on individuals who thought they were going to be enjoying retirement as part of a couple.

More often than not, there is a significant mismatch in the size of the individual retirement provision of the two parties to a marriage or civil partnership. One partner has more money than the other, and that's just the way it is. That's fine if you're going to be growing old together, but none of us knows for sure whether our relationship will stay the course.

We sometimes see one partner get the house and most things in it, but with little financial provision. The other partner might have retained their pension fund, but they have nowhere to live. Both scenarios mean there's some serious catching up to do to provide for a decent retirement.

It is *never* too late

I often find myself repeating this mantra in the YouTube comments section and to email correspondents.

There can be a tendency, if you feel behind due to any of the things we've mentioned, not to bother doing anything about it. It's easy to throw up your hands and say 'well, that's that!' instead of knuckling down to see what *can* be done.

But just a few extra thousand in a pension fund or an ISA can make a difference to the kind of retirement you will enjoy. Just a couple of extra years working, even if it's longer than you hoped, can really turn things around.

Let's look at what can be done if you have some catching up to do.

Everything you need to DO

Get laser focused

If you find yourself divorced in your early 50s, or you are a woman with a retirement provision that is looking a bit anaemic, then it's time to get serious about saving for the future.

There's no magic bullet here, just hard work and sacrifice. You either work hard now so you can make a difference to your future, or you accept the fact that retirement is going to be a bit worse than you'd hoped.

Take a cold, hard look at your budget. Where can you save? How much more can you squeeze out of your monthly income?

Can you ask your boss for a rise? Can you start a side hustle to bring in some more income?

Focus on money coming in and going out so you can find as much disposable income as possible. Now is not the time for frivolous purchases, fancy holidays or spa days – we need to put our money to work.

Look after number one

We talked earlier about the emotional pull of looking after others. This doesn't only apply to women, though they do bear the brunt of it.

If we're going to make a difference to our retirement provision though, we need to start looking after number one.

This is hard, don't mistake me. It might require a frank conversation in which you make your elderly parent aware that you're not going to be able to help them as much as they would like because if you do, your own future is going to be compromised. The same goes for looking after grandchildren – think hard about whether you choose not to work, with all the financial impact of that, so you can babysit for your children's children.

My girls are nowhere near ready to have kids and I've already told them they get one day a week from me and that's it, because I'm going to enjoy my later life and the fruits of my work! Maybe I'm just hard…

Seriously though – no one is going to look out for you better than you will yourself. And if you're starting behind the curve, you're going to need to be strong about this, if you can.

Maximise your efforts

When you've extracted every penny of disposable income you can from your budget, you need to make sure that that money is working as hard as possible.

Prioritise pensions because of the tax relief they attract. Ask about salary sacrifice at work, where you contractually give up some of your income, usually agreed a year at a time, in return for a higher pension contribution. This can save you national insurance and your employer makes a saving too. Some employers will even add the money they save into your pension for you.

If salary sacrifice is not an option, at least ask how much your employers will match when you pay into the pension. Some employers will match your contributions up to a certain level, for example 10% of your earnings. Get the highest match you can from your boss – to do anything else is to leave money on the table.

If you have a Lifetime ISA, you can still contribute up to £4,000 a year into these if you're under 50 years old and there's a 25% government bonus for doing so.

Get aggressive about reducing the costs of your portfolio. Remember that every pound you spend in fees is a pound that isn't compounding for your benefit. Don't make other people rich – look after number one!

Consider the split between partners

If you're in a committed relationship, take a look at the balance of assets between partners. As we've said, more often than not one partner builds up the lion's share of the money.

In the run-up to retirement, you could look to even things up a bit, potentially. Tax-wrapped accounts like pensions and ISAs cannot be transferred between spouses or civil partners, but cash deposits and funds in unwrapped investment accounts like GIAs can.

Tax status is a factor here. If one partner has large pension benefits and is likely to be a higher rate taxpayer in retirement, then there's an argument for shifting the balance of taxable assets into the other partner's name.

As well as moving existing money between partners to even things up a bit, you could consider adding new money in the name of the partner with the smaller portfolio. Chances are that in the run-up to retirement, you're earning the most money you ever have – put this to good use by optimising the split of money between you.

Tax and flexibility are the main reasons to do this, but I've always believed that if one partner has taken a career break to raise children, or if they have been disadvantaged because of illness, then there should be some acknowledgement of this in any healthy partnership. I imagine some readers will disagree with me on this, but I'm seeking to redress the balance for the partner who couldn't work for years, by making pension contributions for them and paying into investments too.

Rethink what's important

If, despite your best efforts, your retirement is going to end up looking different from what you had hoped for, you're going to have to do some thinking and, most likely, you're going to have to lower your expectations.

Perhaps you dreamed of pucker holidays and changing your car every three years in retirement. Perhaps you fantasised about a move to the country to a place with land and a sea view. There's no nice way to say this, but perhaps those things aren't going to happen.

While that's disappointing, no one promised us the perfect life here on Earth. We need to take a Stoic approach and not fret about things we can't do anything about. Instead, we need to focus on what we can control and our outlook on life in general.

Let's focus on what's important. Does it matter what kind of home we live in, or whether we get to eat out once a week or once a month when we retire? Of course not. These things are poor indicators of our general wellbeing anyway, so we mustn't hang our hats on them.

Let's reset our expectations and ground them in the reality of our situation. Let's make the very best of what we have, even if it's less than we'd hoped. Let's look forward to a productive and happy retirement and do our best to make it happen.

Over 11 chapters to this point, we've tried to get a handle on what we have and to maximise our retirement provision heading into retirement.

Now, we arrive at the very threshold of retirement. Let's get ready to dive into the Great Transition.

Phase 2

The Great Transition

HERE WE GO THEN. WE'VE arrived at what we may have felt is the destination, the end goal of all our financial and life planning to this point.

But for most of us, it isn't a single point at all, but a transition into a whole new way of living, where work is optional and new opportunities abound.

It's a little bit scary, but it's pretty exciting too!

Let's get going…

Chapter 12
The Danger Zone

WELL, THAT TITLE IS A bit of a downer, isn't it?! We were all excited to enter retirement and the first thing we see is the word *danger*!

I'm not afraid to admit that I call the early years of retirement the Danger Zone to get people's attention. Just because we're retired now doesn't mean we can take our eyes off the ball.

What ball? Well, two of them actually.

One is that this is the period where you're likely to be drawing the most money from your portfolio and, if not done mindfully, this can damage your wealth irreparably.

And the other is that many people underestimate the emotional impact of the Great Transition into retirement, so it can take a psychological toll too.

So yeah. Two balls. Ahem.

Putting the questionable metaphor aside, we're going to deal with both, erm, factors in this chapter.

By the way, if you've listened to the Meaningful Money podcast, you'll know that I have a habit of playing a burst of Kenny Loggins' iconic song from *Top Gun* – 'Danger Zone' – on the show. I bet you're glad you're reading and not listening to this now!

Everything you need to KNOW

Spending is usually highest in the early years of retirement

If you're anything like most of my clients, you'll already be thinking about how you will spend your time and your money when you retire. That can take many forms because each of us has different dreams and priorities.

If you think about it, the first few years of retirement have the potential to be big-spending years. After all, you are the youngest you're ever going to be in retirement, and with any luck, you'll have the energy and health that goes with that. Also, you're quite likely to be in receipt of one or more cash lump sums from pensions or a business sale.

You also have time on your hands, probably the most free time you've had since you were a child. Free time and available cash is a heady combination! There's no work to get back to, so your holidays can get longer. Long lunches in nice cafes are a possibility more days of the week than before. The camper van you've always promised yourself is not only financially within reach, but you have the time to make use of it.

I tend to find that most new retirees enjoy the ability to spend more freely, even just on the little things – and so they should, they've earned it!

Day-to-day costs don't always rise significantly. Those long lunches are offset by the reduction in commuting costs, perhaps.

Early retirement is definitely an opportunity for one-off costs, though – like whole-family holidays funded by Mum and Dad, changing the car(s) and remodelling the house.

Income is often lowest in the early years of retirement

Conversely, if we retire before state pension age, our actual income is likely to be lower than it will be later in retirement.

Let's say we retire at age 57 and our state pension age is 67. It's quite possible that we have zero income the day after we shake our boss's hand and walk out of the office door for the last time.

We have an old DB pension scheme that kicks in at age 60 with a lump sum in year one. Maybe we have a property that pays us some rent each month. Those will help, sure, but the chances are that we're going to be spending more than those incomes each month.

Maybe at 65 another pension starts to pay out, reducing the amount we need to draw from our pots a bit further. And then at 67 our state pension begins and all our expected incomes are now in payment.

I tend to picture it looking something like in Figure 4. The income sources add up over time, but the white space underneath the Required Spending line is the gap between our incomes and what we need to spend. That gap is largest early on.

Figure 4: The Danger Zone

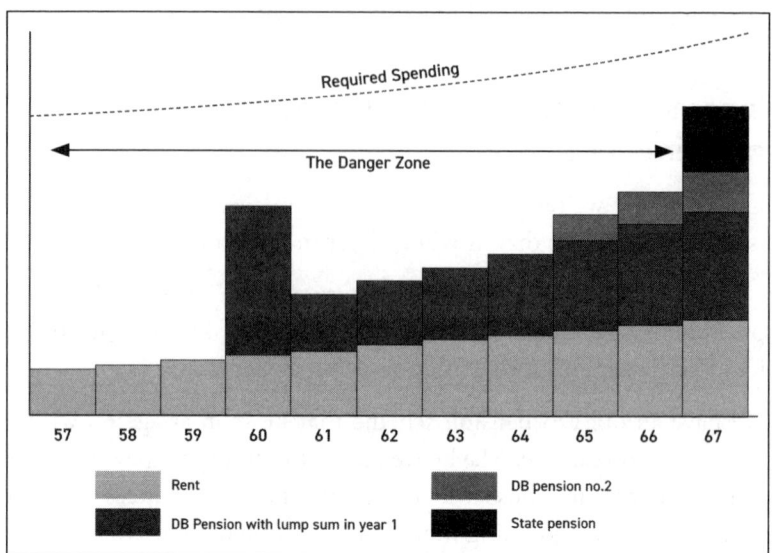

Drawing the most from our cash, pension funds and other investments so early on must be done with careful planning, unless the pots are so big that we're very unlikely to exhaust them.

Most of us don't have unlimited funds, and we want to maximise our enjoyment without risking the possibility of our funds running out. I have a mechanism for that, which we'll cover in detail in Chapter 15.

It can take a while to get used to being retired

Retirement is not just about spending, however. The removal of paid work, whether it happens gradually or all in one go, can be quite a psychological wrench for many of us. This is another reason why I call it the Danger Zone.

Have you noticed that whenever you watch a TV game show where there's an older contestant, they are introduced as a retired fill-in-the-blank?

Chapter 12: The Danger Zone

This is Patricia, and she's a retired headteacher from Nottingham.

Why don't they just say she's retired and having a blast spending the kids' inheritance? Why define her by what she *used* to do for a living?

The fact is we tend to define ourselves by our work. If we meet someone new at an event, one of the first questions we ask is 'and what do you do?' When that work is taken away, we can lose a large part of our identity, potentially leaving a vacuum which needs filling.

Many retirees have plans for how they will fill their time. One recent client who for decades had been at the very top of his field, travelling the world and visiting over a hundred countries, told me that his dream retirement job was to work in the Majestic Wine store across the road from his house. Maybe he was just after the staff discount!

Others will have plans to volunteer at the National Trust or local dog shelter, or dive into helping with the grandchildren.

But lots of people have nothing to go to, and I think this is dangerous. With no focus, the long holiday of retirement has the potential to give rise to depression and loneliness, and that way lies an early grave.

When I first thought about writing this book, I considered making the psychological and emotional challenge of the shift into retirement a central theme. Then I realised I was not even remotely qualified to speak to such matters and that others had done a far better job than I ever could in dealing with the subject.

In the office we keep a few copies of a book called *Changing Gear*, by Jan Hall and Jon Stokes. The subtitle is: *Creating the life you want after a full-on career*. We hand them out to clients where it might be helpful.

Please don't dismiss this element of the Great Transition into retirement. Retirement will be grim without a focus for your life and energy.

With that said, I'm going to revert to what I am good at – the mechanics of financial planning!

Everything you need to DO

Nail down your spending plans

Back in Chapter 4, we spent some time looking at our regular expenditure in the context of setting goals, but now we have arrived at the milestone of retirement, we need to put this in concrete terms.

We also need to consider one-off or irregular costs, and try to look ahead five years or so to what we might need to spend. Would you like to change the car at some point, but maybe not for a year or two? What about that flat roof that needs redoing?

I encourage you to create a written budget. This might be something you haven't done in years, if ever, or maybe you're the kind of person who has always tracked every penny. If you're the latter type, this will be easy.

Create your budget in whatever form works best for you. If you're part of a couple, then do the bulk of this work together.

Think in terms of the three categories:

> **Basic:** Groceries, toiletries, medical/dental costs, fuel for the car, birthday and Christmas gifts, vet bills, phone/internet costs, basic self-care like hairdressing, clothing, committed giving.
>
> **Leisure:** Holidays, clubs and societies, added TV packages, restaurants, entertainment, extra self-care costs.
>
> **Luxury:** Additional holidays, spa days, short breaks, private healthcare, enhanced philanthropy and giving.

Of course, it's your life, so your definition of what falls into which category is the definition that matters, not mine. If you can't imagine life without being able to watch Sky F1, then that's a basic expense for you. (Yes, I'm talking about myself there!)

The three categories will help us prioritise in case things get tight in retirement. The luxury costs would be the ones where we tighten our

Chapter 12: The Danger Zone

belt first, and, in a worst-case scenario, if we need to revert to just the basics, we can.

Try to think about these costs in discrete years. So the basics and leisure costs should be the same in every year, but the luxury costs might be a bit less regular – perhaps we'll go on a long-haul, four-week break every other year, instead of annually.

Think in the same way about the one-off or irregular costs, too. Is the plan to change the car this year, next year or in three years' time? The flat roof needs doing before next winter. Your eldest child might get married at some point in the next five years, but probably not in the next two.

Plot these in a table of numbers as in Table 1.

Table 1: Illustration of annual expenditure over the first five years

	Year 1	Year 2	Year 3	Year 4	Year 5
Basic	£24,000	£24,000	£24,000	£24,000	£24,000
Leisure	£12,000	£12,000	£12,000	£12,000	£12,000
Luxury	£9,000	£19,000 (big holiday)	£9,000	£9,000	£9,000
Irregular	£15,000 (flat roof)	–	£25,000 (change car)	–	£25,000 (child's wedding)
Total	£60,000	£55,000	£70,000	£45,000	£70,000

Always think in today's money when you're working out the costs of things. We know how much the cost of a wedding is today, but we know it's going to be a bit more in future, thanks to inflation.

When planning for clients, I always use a figure of 3% for inflation. Now I know that for 2022 and 2023, inflation was higher than this, but 3% is a decent long-term average.

The maths for inflating figures up into the future is as follows:

$$y = x(1.03)^{(N-1)}$$

where y is the new, inflated figure, x is the starting figure and N is the number of years into the future you want to go.

So if, from Table 1 we want to work out how much the £70,000 we want to spend in year 5 will amount to, the sum is:

$$£70,000 \times (1.03)^4 = £78,785$$

The reason we use N–1 is because we want to spend the money *in* year five, not at the end of it.

If you want to use a spreadsheet to do this, set up your cells like this:

	A	B	C	D
1				
2	Starting amount	Years in the future	Inflation rate	Future value
3	70000	5	3%	=A3*((1+C3)^(B3-1))

Applying this maths to the total of each column in Table 1, we get Table 2.

Table 2: Inflated expenditure over first five years

	Year 1	Year 2	Year 3	Year 4	Year 5
Total costs	£60,000	£55,000	£70,000	£45,000	£70,000
Inflated costs	£60,000	£56,650	£74,263	£49,172	£78,785

This should give you some idea as to just what a big deal inflation is in retirement. Imagine how the numbers will change over 25 years from age 60 to 85!

Chapter 12: The Danger Zone

You can do this exercise over ten years if you like, but the further into the future we look, the more murky things become. We just can't have clarity over those kinds of timescales. You can make assumptions like wanting to change the car every five years, say, but you have no idea about things like repairs or medical bills and such.

Do the same exercise for your incomes

Now we have some idea of what's going out in each year for at least the first five years of our retirement, we need to apply the same kind of logic to our incomes and try to map them into the same kind of table.

Let's say you retire at age 63. For the first two years you plan to do some volunteering, but have no income. Then at age 65, the first of your pensions begins to pay out, at £12,000 a year in today's money. Finally, at age 67, your state pension begins at £11,500 in today's money.

Notice I said 'in today's money'? As both pensions are index-linked, that is, they rise with inflation each year both before and after they start paying out, we need to factor in those rises. We need the figures that would pay out if we were receiving them today and then we need to apply the inflation factors as before.

One more complication – we need to factor in tax, ugh. We do things in this order:

⇨ Start with the income in today's money.

⇨ Apply the inflation factor to that figure.

⇨ Run the future value through a net pay calculator.

I tend to use the net pay calculator at thesalarycalculator.co.uk. Be sure to tick the 'I do not pay National Insurance' box in the additional options section if you're not actually earning an income from a job anymore.

The result would look like Table 3.

Table 3: Calculation of inflation effect on net income

	Year 1 (age 63)	Year 2 (age 64)	Year 3 (age 65)	Year 4 (age 66)	Year 5 (age 67)
Pension 1	–	–	£12,730	£13,112	£13,506
State pension	–	–	–	–	£12,943
Inflated gross income	–	–	£12,730	£13,112	£26,449
Inflated net income	–	–	£12,698	£13,003	£23,673

Now that we have our expenditure and our income expressed in terms that make sense, we can take one away from the other to see what we're going to need our portfolio to provide in each year. Table 4 shows the results.

Table 4: Difference between inflated costs and inflated net income

	Year 1 (age 63)	Year 2 (age 64)	Year 3 (age 65)	Year 4 (age 66)	Year 5 (age 67)
Inflated costs from Table 2	£60,000	£56,650	£74,263	£49,172	£78,785
Inflated net income from Table 3	–	–	£12,698	£13,003	£23,673
Difference	£60,000	£56,650	£61,565	£36,169	£55,112

Chapter 12: The Danger Zone

Don't freak out

Your numbers will be different from those in the tables above, of course. Maybe it all looks very manageable – that's great. But maybe you're looking at your figures and thinking that you're definitely going to need to sell a kidney at some point.

Try not to worry. In my experience, most people that get to retirement age in good financial shape have a decent idea of how much they're going to be able to spend. In fact, most people underestimate to some degree, and I have to spend time encouraging them to spend more or increase their giving.

But maybe you can see why I call this early retirement period the Danger Zone now? In the figures above, our fictional retiree's portfolio would need to be able to supplement their income to the tune of about £270,000 in the first five years.

We need to look now at how to optimise this cash flow that we need to take from our pots.

Chapter 13
Optimising Cash Flow

IF YOU WANT AN ALTERNATIVE title for this chapter, it would be 'What to take from where, and when'. But Optimising Cash Flow is shorter. And it sounds less like a how-to guide for petty theft.

There is no perfect, model retirement plan. Each of us is different, so there is no one-size-fits-all approach. But there's no perfect plan for you, either. At least, not one that can be discerned in advance.

So, we just have to do what we can to look ahead and keep things flexible to take account of changing legislative and taxation rules, as well as our inevitably changing circumstances.

Everything you need to KNOW

We're talking about capital withdrawals here

When I talk about cash flow, I am *combining* income and capital withdrawals.

We've established your sources of income – pensions, annuities, rents and the like. Where there is a gap between our income and our expenses, we must *draw from capital* to make up the difference by taking money out of our portfolio of pensions, ISAs, bank accounts and other stuff.

Capital withdrawal requires us to sell shares or funds, surrender parts of a policy or move money from savings accounts to our current account for spending. Try to keep the distinction between income and capital withdrawals clear in your mind.

Your daily needs are the first priority

It is often said by those in the financial world that you shouldn't let the tax tail wag the investment dog, that is, you shouldn't elevate tax efficiency to a level higher than it deserves, and certainly not above your own comfort and peace of mind. So you should avoid making a subsidiary part of a process the priority. Instead, you should keep things in their proper place.

When establishing the ideal order of withdrawing funds from a portfolio, and reviewing that over time, we mustn't lose sight of the fact that this is not merely an academic exercise. It is a practical process designed to get the money you need to spend into your hands at the right time. If, in so doing, we're not perfectly optimised for tax, then so be it.

The same holds true for other factors of the cash flow process such as your investment approach, which we'll get to in the next chapter, and even estate planning considerations.

First and foremost, you want the money to be there, in your current account, when you need to spend it.

Tax is the next priority

If we're lucky enough to have multiple options from where we could draw the money we need then, yes, tax efficiency is the obvious next factor to consider.

We have several potential sources from which to draw – you will have some or all of these:

- Bank accounts
- National Savings accounts, including Premium Bonds
- DC pension funds
- ISAs
- GIAs
- Investment bonds
- EISs/VCTs
- Downsizing or selling property
- Trust funds.

If we have options, then we should prioritise tax efficiency today, rather than in the future.

For example, as I write, pension funds are deemed to be outside of a person's estate and therefore not subject to inheritance tax, though this is set to change from April 2027. If you have an inheritance tax issue it might make sense to leave your pension funds intact to maximise the impact of that exclusion. But if you are not using your income tax personal allowance *this year* then I would argue that it makes more sense to draw taxable income from your pension within that allowance than to leave it unused.

Common sense will prevail

There has been a great deal of work done by far brighter minds than mine over the years in the field of retirement income strategies. This work has led to all kinds of methods for optimising cash flow, the investment of a portfolio and the like.

One of the most famous to emerge is the concept of spending guardrails. What this means is that you can establish some rules for your spending patterns, and it has been shown that these can significantly increase the likelihood of your portfolio outliving you.

For example, you could say that if the value of your portfolio increases by 20%, you will increase your spending accordingly, perhaps by the same proportion. On the other hand, if the portfolio falls by 20%, you could decrease your spending by that proportion. I've never met anyone who opted to reduce spending by the same percentage as the fall in their portfolio value. Rather, they will choose to reduce by a smaller amount, say 5%.

These guardrails are often hard boundaries – so if the portfolio grows by 19% you only increase your spending by the usual inflationary rise and not by 19%; and if the portfolio falls by 19% you could just choose to maintain your spending at the current rate.

The most famous proponents of these types of guardrails are Jonathan Guyton and William Klinger, whose original paper on this subject is freely available for download.[17]

In practice, though, I find that in the vast majority of cases, people already have the skills they need to manage their response to changing economic conditions. All the good discipline they have brought to bear in getting to the point of having enough money to retire doesn't then desert them the second they cross the line into retirement.

I will often have conversations, perhaps at a client's annual review when markets are distressed, where the client will decide to postpone a large withdrawal until things recover a bit. This common-sense approach has served them well for decades, and still will in retirement.

For all our efforts to optimise things, let's not go so deep as to lose ourselves in detail. We need to keep things simple. Remember, there is no perfect approach except the one known in hindsight. If we do our best and keep our heads, we'll be OK.

That said, let's get practical.

Chapter 13: Optimising Cash Flow

Everything you need to DO

Consider an annuity

Remember, your current needs are a priority. Remember, too, that we have grouped our expenses into basic, leisure and luxury priorities so we could tighten our belts in the right places if necessary.

So if your basic expenses are not met throughout life by existing secured income, then you should think about addressing that.

I use the term *secured income* to mean income that is pretty much guaranteed to be received: DB pensions, state pensions, existing annuities, trust fund income and maybe rent from an investment property.

It might be that we'll have to dip into capital to cover our basic expenses while we're in the Danger Zone (cue Kenny Loggins!), but ideally, once we get to state pension age, we would like all of our basic expenditure to be covered by guaranteed sources of income.

If there is a shortfall, then it's worth looking at annuities to bridge the gap.

The Government's Money Helper site has a page where you can enter your details and receive live quotes from annuity providers.[18]

Think through whether you need a lifetime annuity or a temporary one, and if there are two of you, think about how to structure the annuity in case one of you dies. Would the other one still need the full income? Costs for one person would likely be lower, so there's no point in providing an income that the survivor wouldn't actually need.

Annuities are taxed as income, so you may need to factor in income tax.

For example, if you already have an income over the personal allowance, then you're going to pay 20% income tax on any annuity you set up. If the annuity income, when added to your other income, takes you over £50,270 for the year, then you're going to be a higher rate taxpayer and pay 40% tax on some of the annuity income. Income tax is taken at source from annuities, so you will get the net amount paid into your bank account.

The peace of mind that comes from knowing that your basic needs will be met for life is powerful. In buying an annuity you will be handing over a chunk of your capital, but I think this is the first thing we should check when we are planning our cash flow needs.

Think about tax-efficient drawing in order

Turning now to withdrawing from our capital, we need to think about the tax implications in doing so.

When deciding where best to draw from to supplement a client's retirement income, I find it helpful to think in terms of an order of tax efficiency.

Start with income that can be tax free:

> **Use your personal allowance.** Use this first if you can. Be aware of income from pensions, as well as interest and dividends from shares or funds held outside of a pension or ISA. If part of your personal allowance is going unused, see if you can draw from otherwise taxable sources like a pension to use it up.
>
> **Draw down pension tax-free cash.** You can use this as part of a regular plan of drawing from a pension by using regular UFPLS payments. A quarter of each payment will be tax free with the other three-quarters being taxable, and perhaps falling within the personal allowance noted above. Or you could just take a tax-free cash lump sum.
>
> **Use the annual exempt allowance.** You could sell assets within the capital gains tax AEA and pay no tax on the transaction. These need to be assets which are *not* held in a pension or ISA.
>
> **Use the 5% withdrawal facility on an investment bond.** This has no immediate implications for income tax, but once all of the original investment has been withdrawn, you might have

to start paying tax. But usually, you can stop the withdrawals at that point.

Draw from cash. There's no tax to pay when drawing your own money out of the bank or building society.

Once you have exhausted the tax-free options, look at incurring tax carefully:

Capital gains tax. This is currently (tax year 2024/25) charged at 18% for basic rate taxpayers and 24% for higher and additional rate taxpayers (more when you're selling property). Perhaps you could sell down parts of your portfolio which are subject to this tax.

Investment bonds. If you have an investment bond you could draw from this in excess of the 5% permitted withdrawals. You'll incur some income tax, but only if you become a higher rate taxpayer as a result of the withdrawal. If the bond is of the offshore variety, you will incur basic and potentially higher rate income tax.

Draw from pension funds. You will pay income tax, but you should look to stay within the basic rate band if possible.

It's worth mentioning that if you're part of a couple, you should think about this for both of you. If the choice comes down to incurring higher rate income tax for one partner, while the other one would only pay basic rate tax for drawing down the same amount, then you would opt for the latter where possible.

Tax isn't to be avoided at all costs – it is an inevitable part of having income and capital – but we might as well play the game well, and not incur *unnecessary* tax.

Tax is just another cost; it's a drag on your portfolio returns and will hasten the day when the money runs out. With some careful tax optimisation, you can push that day back.

Don't hold too much cash

Many people have a tendency to hold lots of cash when they are retired. As we'll see in Chapter 15, you should only hold cash for two reasons:

> **As an emergency fund**. How much this amounts to is up to you, but it's the figure that you're comfortable knowing you can write a cheque for from tomorrow. It is 'sleep-at-night' money. Pretty much all your assets will be realisable, given enough time, and potentially at the cost of paying a ton of tax. But your emergency fund is there for you *now*, in case you need it.

> **The next two years' expenses**. I'm going to propose that, where possible, you always have the next two years' worth of expenses held in cash. This doesn't have to be in the bank. It could be held in cash within your ISAs and pensions, but the idea is that this money is *not* invested, it isn't at risk. All will become clear, I promise!

In any normal situation, money in the bank will attract interest at less than the rate of inflation. This means you are losing money on everything you keep there – that's reason enough to keep it to a minimum.

Hopefully you're starting to think in terms of an order of operations. So far we have:

⇨ Work out your expenses for the next five years.

⇨ Know when your various sources of income are coming in and how much they amount to, so you can work out the shortfall in each year.

⇨ Fill that shortfall by drawing from capital each year, according to the priority list above. Try to be tax efficient where possible.

We will get to a point where we have a good idea which of our pots are going to be bridging our income/expense gap each year.

Knowing that, we can begin to look at how the money in those pots is invested.

Chapter 14
Investing Options

IT'S FUNNY HOW PRESENTING A podcast and a YouTube channel for years helps you to distil big subjects down to just a sentence or two. It forces you to continually refine your presentation, to find better ways of expressing things.

What is investing, really? Now whenever I am asked this question, or it comes up on the show, I answer it like this:

> Investing is swapping your cash for assets which increase in value, produce an income, or ideally both.

We have two strings to our metaphorical bow when investing – capital returns and income. When the two combine – we call that *total return* – that's when the magic of compounding really kicks in and does great work on our behalf.

The *purpose* of investing is to beat inflation and preserve the buying power of our money into the future.

I want to look at the main approaches to investment so you can think about how they might fit into your plans.

Everything you need to KNOW

Income investing

In the accumulation phase of our lives, when we are working and building towards our eventual retirement, income produced by our portfolio is usually reinvested. But when we do retire, it might be useful to have that money available to spend instead.

Income is derived in three main ways:

> **Interest.** This is produced by money held on deposit, or the coupon paid by corporate and government bonds, including bond funds.
>
> **Dividends.** This is the investors' share of the profits made by a company.
>
> **Rent.** This is paid by tenants of a property we own.

Where the asset producing the income is inside a tax wrapper, then how the income is treated is dictated by the wrapper itself. So if you have shares in an ISA and they produce a dividend, then the income will be tax free in your hands. If the dividend is produced by shares held in your pension fund, then if you choose to take the income out of the pension, the usual rules for taxation will apply.

Because we usually hold our assets inside funds, how the income is handled by the fund depends on the type of fund we hold, of which there are two main options:

> **Accumulation funds (usually suffixed with 'Acc').** Here the income is produced and is used to increase the price of the shares in the fund. In simple terms, if the fund share price is £10 and the dividend produced is 40p, then the share price becomes £10.40. The income isn't paid out, as such, it just gets absorbed into the share price.

Income funds (suffixed with 'Inc,' or 'Dis,' for distribution). Here the income is spun out into cash. You can either opt for the cash to buy more shares or have it paid out to you.

Yield, bonds and equities

The income produced by an investment is usually expressed as a percentage figure, the *yield* of the asset. So if you invest £100 into something with a 4% yield, you can expect it to produce an income of about £4 per year.

There is a link between yield and the riskiness of the asset producing it, but it tends to work differently with bonds and equities.

If we look at equities first, companies that produce a consistent, predictable dividend income tend to be larger, well-established companies in sectors such as finance, pharmaceuticals and energy. These are companies whose share price is unlikely to skyrocket, so the dividend yield is a key reason that investors buy the shares.

Companies that are more about growth may not pay much of a dividend, if at all. Investors buy these companies in the hope of increasing the value of their holding. Often these are smaller companies, and hence have a higher chance of failing, but sometimes they are the biggest companies in the world, often in the technology sector.

Very generally, a growth company might expect its share price to be more volatile in the pursuit of that growth, whereas a company producing a dividend might expect its share price to be fairly non-volatile, but will focus on making strong profits and distributing them via dividends. So you get a higher yield from less volatile shares.

With bonds, the link between risk and yield is usually reversed.

Bonds are issued by companies and governments looking to raise money. If they are deemed a sure bet to pay the interest on the bond and repay the capital on time, then they won't have to offer a particularly attractive interest rate to attract investors.

If the company or government is smaller, more likely to default on the bond or even fail altogether, then they will need to boost the interest rate on the bond to attract investors.

The Vietnamese government, say, is likely to offer higher rates on their bonds than the UK government, for example. And if a smaller company were issuing a bond, they'd have to offer a higher interest rate than, say, Vodafone would, to reflect the fact that they're a higher risk than Vodafone. Figure 5 illustrates this point.

Figure 5: The bond yield/quality scale

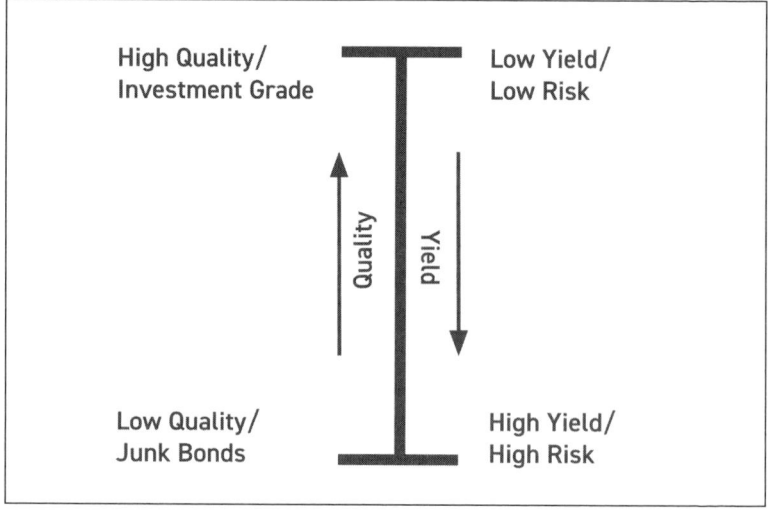

So with bonds, the higher the quality of the issuer, the lower the yield will be, and vice versa.

You need to understand this when looking at a high-yield bond fund, for example. The high-yield part of the name sounds attractive, but there will be a higher risk of price volatility, too.

Income is variable

I think it is really important for retiring investors to remember that income is variable. When you deposit cash with a bank or building society for a couple of years, you get a fixed rate of interest. However, when you're investing for income, you can expect that income to fluctuate, and sometimes significantly.

With dividends produced by shares, if something comes along that threatens a company or the sector it sits within, then the board of that company may decide to sit on more cash for a while, and reduce or even cancel their dividend programme. At the same time, that threat might lead to a decline in the share price of the company, so the value of your holding will fall at the same time as your income is reduced.

With bonds, the income is fixed by definition, but only if you buy and hold a bond directly. As most of us use funds for our investments, the fund manager will buy and sell bonds at different times. While their goal is to maintain a decent level of income and protect the fund share price, there is still the likelihood that the income will fluctuate, though probably not a great deal.

You may need to factor this potential variability into your planning, so be aware.

Total return investing

Total return investing is using the combination of both income and capital value increases to grow your wealth. In retirement, the idea is that the total return will be enough to cover any withdrawals you need to make.

Even if you do still erode your portfolio over time by drawing out more than it makes, a decent total return should prolong the longevity of your portfolio for as long as possible.

You can balance the income and capital return elements of a portfolio by adjusting its asset allocation. This term refers to how your portfolio is divided between asset types or geographical locations, or even a combination of the two.

If we simplify asset allocation for our purposes to mean the split between equities and bonds, then consider the four portfolios shown in Figure 6.

Figure 6: Four portfolios with different asset allocations

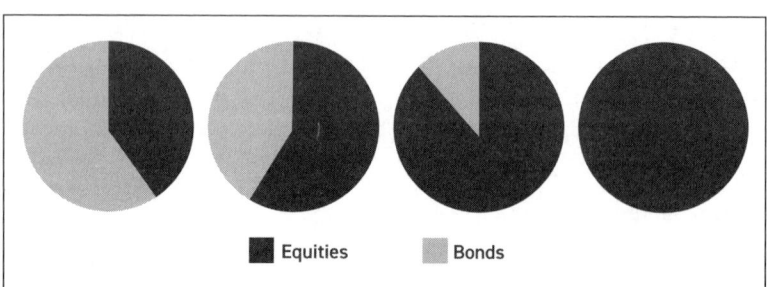

From left to right, I would call these Cautious (40% equities), Balanced (60% equities), Growth (80% equities) and Adventurous (100% equities).

Generally, more cautious investors hold more bonds than adventurous investors. Likewise, it's likely that an investor looking for more predictable income would opt for more bonds, too.

Taking those splits between equities and bonds, assuming they are rebalanced once a year, and choosing a Vanguard global equity fund and a global bond fund, the income yields for the portfolios would look like those in Table 5.

Table 5: Current yield figures as at 18 April 2024

	Cautious	Balanced	Growth	Adventurous
Yield	3.45%	2.86%	2.28%	1.69%

On this basis, you could get more than twice the income from the 40% equity (Cautious) portfolio than from the 100% equity (Adventurous) portfolio.

Looking at the capital return of the same portfolios gives the results shown in Table 6, at least over the last approximately eight years that the Vanguard funds I've chosen have been in existence.

Table 6: Capital returns for the four portfolios, 24 February 2016 to 18 April 2024; returns not inflation adjusted

	Cautious	Balanced	Growth	Adventurous
Simple average annual capital return	5.25%	8.20%	11.54%	15.29%

And finally, Table 7 shows the total return, where the income yield is reinvested into the relevant portfolio.

Table 7: Income yield reinvested for the four portfolios, 24 February 2016 to 18 April 2024; returns not inflation adjusted

	Cautious	Balanced	Growth	Adventurous
Average annual total return	9.69%	12.79%	16.22%	19.98%

Let's put some pounds and pence figures onto this. Let's assume an investment of £100,000 made on 24 February 2016, which is when the funds I've chosen began, and assume also that 4% of the portfolio value at the start of each year is withdrawn every year, taken monthly on the first of every month. Table 8 shows the results after eight years and two months.

Table 8: Value of investment of £100,000 as at 18 April 2024, 4% withdrawn pa, taken monthly; investment made on 24 February 2016; returns not inflation adjusted

	Cautious	Balanced	Growth	Adventurous
Closing balance	£128,315	£146,452	£166,460	£188,457

Now, of course, every period you choose will deliver a different result, but the period here includes the Covid-19 pandemic and the very challenging conditions stemming from high inflation and interest rates.

What's the lesson here? While income yield is helpful, it usually comes at the price of much lower capital returns over any meaningful timescale.

In this example, you would have more of the income you need guaranteed by the natural yield of the Cautious portfolio, but by opting for the Adventurous approach, you would have had some income, plus bagged an extra £60,000 of return.

I *always* recommend a total return approach to my clients. Most people simply don't have enough capital to be able to rely entirely on the natural yield of their portfolio and ignore the capital returns.

The majority of my clients need some capital return working for them to make their plans work. And that's especially true in the early years of their retirement – the Danger Zone.

Also, most of them are keen to leave what they can for their children and grandchildren, and a total return approach gives them the best chance of maximising their legacy.

Finally, remember back in Chapter 4 when we discussed how big a deal inflation is in retirement? If you strip out the income from the returns of your portfolio, what's left has a lower chance of outpacing inflation.

Sequence of returns risk

This is turning out to be the mother of all KNOW sections, isn't it? Last bit here, I promise.

A big risk when it comes to withdrawing money from your portfolio in retirement is the so-called sequence of returns risk, sometimes called sequencing risk. Investopedia defines this as:

> Sequence risk is the danger that the timing of withdrawals from a retirement account will have a negative impact on the overall rate of return available to the investor. This can have a significant impact on a retiree who depends on the income from a lifetime of investing and is no longer contributing new capital that could offset losses.

If you need to draw from your portfolio when the investments in it are distressed, then you could do significant damage to the portfolio, from which it may never fully recover.

If you're lucky enough to retire right as markets begin a nice long upward run, that's great. But if markets fall for three consecutive years right as you need to start drawing off your portfolio, then you could significantly shorten the life of your portfolio. It could make the difference between you running out of money one day and having some left to leave to the kids.

As we can't know the future, there is no way to avoid sequence of returns risk altogether, but we can take certain steps to reduce its impact.

Everything you need to DO

Think about your options

Maybe you already have a clear view of how you like to invest, maybe you don't. When you retire, chances are you're going to be dependent on the performance of your portfolio to maintain your lifestyle, so your investment approach is vitally important.

If you were thinking to rely on the natural income of your portfolio to supplement your other income sources without dipping into the capital itself, do you have enough? Are you prepared to largely forget about the capital value of your portfolio and focus purely on the income?

Or were you planning to leave things largely as you have done while accumulating, keeping things simple and hoping for the best in terms of returns?

It is impossible to know what the best approach will be for you and your timescale and the point in history that you are retiring, but we will be able to review and change things if needed as we go along. That means any investment choices we make as we enter retirement don't have to be set-and-forget, which should take the pressure off a little bit.

Build a cash flow ladder

The cash flow ladder is the mechanism we use to harness the power of total return investing while seeking to minimise the impact of sequence of returns risk.

This merits its own chapter, so your to-do here is simply to keep reading!

Chapter 15
The Cash Flow Ladder

LET'S HAVE A VERY QUICK RECAP:

Inflation is a huge risk factor in retirement. If we want to maintain our lifestyle, we need our income and withdrawals to at least be maintained in real terms.

Costs and tax are a drag on our portfolio returns.

Total return investing offers two strings to our bow in the battle against inflation.

Sequence of returns risk means that our need for withdrawals might work against us if markets are also distressed when we need the money.

We need to keep our money invested, but we need to do so intentionally. It's not true to say that you should be invested more cautiously in retirement than when you're building wealth. This is because it's likely that your portfolio will need to work harder than ever once you're dependent on it for your lifestyle needs.

It's quite the balancing act, really. Managing spending, costs, tax and investment returns sounds like hard work, but it doesn't have to be. The cash flow ladder is designed to be set up, then reviewed just once a year.

Let's get into it.

Everything you need to KNOW and DO

In a break from tradition, I'm going to blend the KNOW and DO sections here and we're going to work through an example so you can see how the ladder is built.

Two years' spending in cash

Meet Jane and Chris. Jane is 59 and Chris is 56. They are standing on the cusp of retiring and are looking to make sure they are drawing the right money from the right places at the right time. They have money in the bank and each has a DC pension and a stocks and shares ISA.

They need to spend £45,000 a year to enjoy a decent lifestyle including one annual summer holiday and a couple of city breaks. They have recently changed their car, and they'd like to do so roughly every five years.

They decide to keep £25,000 in an emergency fund, completely separate from their wider portfolio.

The first thing they need to do is to make sure they have the first two years' spending in cash, whether that's in the bank or in their pensions and ISAs.

Why two years' worth of cash? Studies have shown that a blended portfolio has recovered to its previous high within two years in about 95% of cases.[19]

Jane and Chris have no income now that they have retired, so they're well and truly in the Danger Zone.

Table 9 looks at how they could structure things.

Chapter 15: The Cash Flow Ladder

Table 9: Example of how to structure retirement finances in the first two years

	Total needed	Jane pension	Jane ISA	Chris pension	Chris ISA	Bank	Risk profile
Year 2	£45,000	£16,760	–	£16,760	–	£11,480	Risk-free
Year 1	£45,000	£16,760	–	£16,760	–	£11,480	

Note the emergency fund is not included here

As they have no income at the moment, it makes sense to use their income tax personal allowances. They do this by taking an UFPLS payment from each of their pension funds of £16,760. Of this, £4,190 will be tax-free cash, with the remaining £12,570 falling within their personal allowance.

The balance of the £45,000 needed is £11,480 and they could take this from their bank account.

They have met their cash flow needs without paying any tax – a good result.

We can simplify the bottom two rungs of the ladder, as shown in Table 10.

Table 10: Simplifying the first two years

	Total needed	Jane pension	Jane ISA	Chris pension	Chris ISA	Bank	Risk profile
Years 1–2	£90,000	£33,520	–	£33,520	–	£22,960	Risk-free

Now we can see how much Jane and Chris need to keep in cash *inside* their pensions. No sense in risking this money, I would argue. We know we're going to need it soon, so it should stay in cash.

Important note: To keep things simple here, I'm going to ignore inflation. As we go up the ladder to the longer timescales, we should apply some multiplier to the cash needed each year. I'm going to simplify things for you shortly, so that you don't really need to worry about inflation for your own planning. Also, I'm assuming that figures are after tax. I want to get across the principles and not get too bogged down with weird numbers and tax calculations.

Years 3–5 – Should be invested more cautiously than your standard risk profile.

Let's say that things continue like this, but in year 5 Jane and Chris would like to earmark £20,000 to change their car. This means that in that year, they will need to spend £65,000.

Maybe they continue with their pensions as they did in years 1–2 but now they start to use their ISAs. Table 11 illustrates the numbers.

Table 11: Moving into years 3–5

	Total needed	Jane pension	Jane ISA	Chris pension	Chris ISA	Bank	Risk profile
Year 5	£65,000	£16,760	£15,740	£16,760	£15,740	–	Risk – Cautious
Year 4	£45,000	£16,760	£5,740	£16,760	£5,740	–	
Year 3	£45,000	£16,760	£5,740	£16,760	£5,740	–	
Years 1–2	£90,000	£33,520	–	£33,520	–	£22,960	Risk-free

Note that I suggest that money for years 3–5 should be invested, at outset, according to a 'Risk-' or 'Risk-Minus' profile. This means a step *down* from their ordinary risk profile. So if Jane and Chris are normally Balanced investors, then the money for years 3–5 would be invested with a Cautious approach.

Chapter 15: The Cash Flow Ladder

Again, we can simplify to show how much money should be invested at the Risk-Minus level in each account, as shown in Table 12.

Table 12: Simplified version of Table 11

	Total needed	Jane pension	Jane ISA	Chris pension	Chris ISA	Bank	Risk profile
Years 3–5	£155,000	£50,280	£27,220	£50,280	£27,220	–	Risk - Cautious
Years 1–2	£90,000	£33,520	–	£33,520	–	£22,960	Risk-free

Years 6–10 – Invested according to standard risk profile

In year 6, Jane has a DB pension kicking in of £14,000 a year. She's now a taxpayer, so they'll need to rethink things a little bit.

In year 8, Jane turns 67 and her state pension begins – let's say this is £11,000 a year.

Firstly, they don't need to draw £45,000 a year from the portfolio anymore. In years 6 and 7, they will just need £31,000 and from year 8 onwards, just £20,000.

But in year 10, they will want to change the car again, and this time they want to earmark £30,000, so we'll need £50,000 in that year. Table 13 shows how the cash flow ladder might look.

Table 13: Cash flow ladder in years 6–10

	Total needed	Jane pension	Jane ISA	Chris pension	Chris ISA	Bank	Risk profile
Year 10	£50,000	–	£16,620	£16,760	£16,620	–	
Year 9	£20,000	–	£1,620	£16,760	£1,620	–	
Year 8	£20,000	–	£1,620	£16,760	£1,620	–	Risk = Balanced
Year 7	£31,000	–	£7,120	£16,760	£7,120	–	
Year 6	£31,000	–	£7,120	£16,760	£7,120	–	
Years 3–5	£155,000	£50,280	£27,220	£50,280	£27,220	–	Risk - Cautious
Years 1–2	£90,000	£33,520	–	£33,520	–	£22,960	Risk-free

As Jane is now a taxpayer, it doesn't make sense to draw taxable income from her DC pension, though she could opt to draw some tax-free cash each year.

As Chris still doesn't have any income, he can keep drawing in the same way from his pension, without paying income tax.

The ISAs will continue to fund the shortfall each year.

Money for years 6–10 should be invested according to the couple's *standard risk profile* – Balanced, in this case.

Again, we can simplify the ladder into broad stages, so we can see what needs to be invested at this risk profile in each account. Table 14 shows a simplified version of Table 13.

Chapter 15: The Cash Flow Ladder

Table 14: Simplified version of Table 13

	Total needed	Jane pension	Jane ISA	Chris pension	Chris ISA	Bank	Risk profile
Years 6–10	£152,000	–	£34,100	£83,800	£34,100	–	Risk = Balanced
Years 3–5	£155,000	£50,280	£27,220	£50,280	£27,220	–	Risk - Cautious
Years 1–2	£90,000	£33,520	–	£33,520	–	£22,960	Risk-free

Year 11+ – push the investment harder

We have just one more rung to add to our ladder. I'm not going to worry about what income is coming in when this is so far into the future. We're simply going to say that any other money that we haven't already accounted for sits on this rung of the ladder. Table 15 draws everything together.

Table 15: Years 1 to 11+ summary

	Total needed	Jane pension	Jane ISA	Chris pension	Chris ISA	Bank	Risk profile
Years 11+		EVERYTHING ELSE					Risk + Growth
Years 6–10	£152,000	–	£34,100	£83,800	£34,100	–	Risk = Balanced
Years 3–5	£155,000	£50,280	£27,220	£50,280	£27,220	–	Risk - Cautious
Years 1–2	£90,000	£33,520	–	£33,520	–	£22,960	Risk-free

This money should be invested one notch *above* the couple's standard risk profile. As Jane and Chris are Balanced investors, we're going to go for a Growth approach here.

We have identified that the couple needs £397,000 to get them through the first ten years of retirement. As it happens in our example, Chris's state pension kicks in in year 11, as does a small public sector DB scheme. After this, the couple will only need to dip into their capital to fund car purchases and other ad hoc expenses, such as gifts to their family.

Building the cash flow ladder – investing choices

Now that we have a sense of how much we need to spend out of each pot, we can think about how to achieve the investment approaches *inside* those pots.

Let's take Chris's pension as our example, and let's assume that it has a balance of a nice, round £300,000. Looking at the ladder we have designed, that £300k needs investing as shown in Table 16.

Table 16: Chris's pension investments

	Risk profile	Chris pension
Years 11+	Risk + Growth	£132,400
Years 6–10	Risk = Balanced	£83,800
Years 3–5	Risk – Cautious	£50,280
Years 1–2	Risk-free	£33,520

Professional advisers have access to platforms and pension providers which allow them to create sub-accounts for their clients. One pension plan for Chris could therefore have three sub-accounts and a cash account. Each sub-account can then be invested along one of the risk profiles.

But as I write, I don't know of any direct-to-consumer platforms that have this functionality.

You could achieve the same thing with four different pension plans, but this seems like an unnecessary complication, and would certainly make it difficult to move money between the rungs of the ladder. Instead, I suggest you achieve the split of investments by choosing different funds at each level.

You may have heard of the Vanguard LifeStrategy range of funds. They are off-the-shelf, done-for-you portfolio funds which come in different flavours: 20%, 40%, 60%, 80% and 100% equities.

Note, this is not a recommendation, just an example – there are other such funds available from different providers!

We could set up Chris's pension using these Vanguard funds, as shown in Table 17.

Table 17: Chris's pensions using Vanguard funds as an example

	Risk profile	Chris pension	Fund
Years 11+	Risk + Growth	£132,400	Vanguard LifeStrategy 80% Equity fund
Years 6–10	Risk = Balanced	£83,800	Vanguard LifeStrategy 60% Equity fund
Years 3–5	Risk – Cautious	£50,280	Vanguard LifeStrategy 40% Equity fund
Years 1–2	Risk-free	£33,520	Cash account

This keeps each rung of the ladder separate and maintains a consistent investment approach. You could, of course, choose entirely different funds at each rung. You could also have more than one fund at each rung. As long as you know which funds belong at which risk level, you're good to go.

Now maybe you are thinking that if we ignore the cash rung, then we could just average out the other rungs and get about 66% equity content across those funds. Why not just find a fund that has 66% equity or somewhere close and simplify the whole thing to just one fund and some cash?

You certainly could do this, but the ladder is a behavioural tool as much as a mechanism for minimising sequence of returns risk. Knowing that you can largely ignore the top rung of the ladder – because you're not going to access it for ten years – goes a long way to simplifying and reducing the number of things you have to think about when managing your portfolio.

Really, once the ladder is set up, all you have to do is to review the split of funds each year or so and make sure there's enough accessible cash for at least the next year or two.

You can see, I hope, that having multiple pension plans and ISAs etc. would make creating and reviewing a cash flow ladder prohibitively complex. Maybe you get a kick out of that sort of thing, but I know I don't! Even doing this professionally for our clients, I am always looking for ways to simplify without compromising security or peace of mind. Usually, that means fewer accounts and fewer funds than you might think.

Reviewing the cash flow ladder

Let's say that Jane and Chris set up their ladder and get on with enjoying their retirement together. Soon enough, the first anniversary of their retirement rolls around, and they sit down to review things.

They are now a year down the line, so the amount of cash in the bank and in their pension pots – the first rung of the ladder – should have halved.

If it is our goal always to keep two years of cash on hand, then we need to top up this bottom rung if we can.

Remember that the idea of this two-year block of cash is to minimise the chance of us having to sell down assets while they are distressed.

At review time, there are likely two outcomes: the other funds have made a profit, or they are currently sitting at a loss.

If the rest of the portfolio is currently sitting on a loss, that's why we have two years' worth of cash on hand. We can defer the review of the ladder and come back to it in six months or a year's time when hopefully the situation has improved. In the meantime, we carry on as we are, spending down the second year of cash as planned.

If the funds are sitting on a profit, we need to rebuild the ladder, starting on the bottom rung and working up.

Working from the bottom up means that our first job is to top up the cash element. We can take this from any of the other three rungs. In buoyant markets, it's likely that the top rung will have performed better, so it might be tempting to take all your profit from there and shift it to the bottom rung.

But we're working from the bottom up. So if the years 3–5 rung is sitting on some profit over and above what you are now going to need for that time period, then take the profit from there first.

If there's not enough profit there to top up the cash, then move one step up the ladder to the years 6–10 rung and use any profit there. Finally, move to the top rung and take what you need from there.

Here are the steps:

1. Determine how much you need to top up the cash rung
2. Work out how much money you need in the years 3–5 rung of the ladder now that you're a year down the line. Anything in those funds in excess of that figure, move it to the bottom rung.
3. Do the same exercise for the years 6–10 rung of the ladder.
4. Finally, if you still need to find more cash, move up to the year 11+ rung and take what you need from there.

Working this way means that the more aggressively invested money gets touched last, leaving it to do its thing and grow into the future. The nearer-term money is the stuff that is being worked and remoulded as you rebuild the ladder each year.

If you have kept things simple and have one fund at each rung of the ladder, then all you're going to end up doing is placing some sell trades from the funds to top up the cash buffer.

What if the difficult markets last more than two years?

If you get to the end of two years and you're still sitting on losses, and you're getting to the end of your cash, what should you do?

In this case, you're going to need to spend what was year 3's money no matter what, so you are going to have to reconcile yourself to selling some funds for little gain, or maybe even for a loss.

I tend to switch to a more regular review process when this happens, selling down, say, three months' spending needs from the years 3–5 rung and dropping that into cash you can spend.

In three months' time, sit down again. Maybe things are looking a little better. If so, is there any profit in the higher rungs you can drop down to the cash buffer? Still work from the bottom up, taking profit from the lower rungs first.

If things are looking bleak, sell down another three months' worth of spending needs and then sit down again.

In due course, things will improve – they always do. But by selling smaller portions of the invested money every three months or so, you're only taking a relatively small amount out of the benefit of rising markets when they come.

Simplified ladders

There's a chance that you're thinking that all this still sounds like too much work. It is possible to simplify things further and still get the benefit of reducing the impact of sequence of returns risk.

Chapter 15: The Cash Flow Ladder

Tables 18 and 19 show two examples, using a three-rung ladder and a two-rung ladder respectively.

Three-rung ladder

Table 18 shows Jane and Chris's situation again, but this time split into just three rungs.

Table 18: Using a three-rung ladder

	Total needed	Jane pension	Jane ISA	Chris pension	Chris ISA	Bank	Risk profile
Years 9+	EVERYTHING ELSE						Risk + Growth
Years 4–8	£192,000	£33,520	£37,340	£83,800	£37,340	–	Risk = Balanced
Years 1–3	£135,000	£50,280	£5,740	£50,280	£5,740	£22,960	Risk-free

In this situation, we've kept a cash buffer of three years' spending rather than just two. We've also eliminated the Risk-Minus rung of the ladder and gone straight to Risk-Equals. The logic there is that if we have a larger cash buffer we can take a bit more risk with the invested portion.

Certainly, this would require less work at review time. It's less nuanced, but maybe that's a good thing! It's even more likely that the invested portion would have recovered in three years rather than two, meaning that we're unlikely to have to resort to the three shorter-term reviews' schedule we discussed earlier.

Two-rung ladder

I'm quite certain that something with just two rungs can't accurately be called a ladder. Perhaps a step-stool? Anyway, this really is the simplest way of protecting against sequence of returns risk, as shown in Table 19.

Table 19: Using a two-rung ladder

	Total needed	Jane pension	Jane ISA	Chris pension	Chris ISA	Bank	Risk profile
Years 6+	EVERYTHING ELSE						Risk = Balanced
Years 1–5	£245,000	£83,800	£27,220	£83,800	£27,220	£22,960	Risk-free

Here we have a five-year cash buffer (you could choose three or four years if you prefer) and everything else is invested according to Jane and Chris's balanced risk profile.

Keeping so much cash is a drag on returns, of course, and much depends on exactly how much 'everything else' adds up to. There is an assumption that there is enough money invested to last for the rest of your life, with a fair wind in markets and some continued prudence in spending.

Whether or not you have enough is a very difficult question to answer without powerful modelling software. My experience is that if a client is cutting it fine, there is a chance they may run out of capital later in life. If this appears to be the case, then the more nuanced and careful version of the ladder shown in Table 15 will serve them better. If there's plenty of money on hand, then just opt for one of the simpler versions – keep enough cash and invest the rest in one or two rungs.

In this lengthy chapter we've looked at the investment lever that we can control to give our portfolio the best chance of outliving us. But there is one more lever which we need to discuss – our spending.

Chapter 16
Managing Spending Patterns

THE AMOUNT OF MONEY WE spend each month or each year is easily the most effective lever we have in our control when it comes to affecting our financial outcomes.

When we are accumulating wealth, the better control we have over our spending, the better the outcome is likely to be. We won't waste money, we will save regularly and see our net worth grow.

When it comes to retirement, we should still keep our hands firmly on this lever, while still enjoying all the benefits that being retired has to offer.

Everything you need to KNOW

Humans like patterns

Over my 25+ year career, I've spotted several universal truths about the way people handle their finances. They're universal in that they apply to everyone, rich or poor, and one of the most pertinent to our discussions is that humans like regularity of income.

I'm not a psychologist so I have no idea why this is the case, but surely it has to do with the fact that most of us get paid the same amount of money on the same date every month. From my earliest days as a paperboy this was the case – the conditioning towards a regular income started early!

When we retire, our regular income from earnings stops for good. To some extent that can be replaced by the state pension or DB pension schemes. Maybe we have rent coming in every month from a tenanted property, too.

The majority of us are going to need to dip into capital to supplement that income. That's what the whole preceding chapter was about – managing the investments so that the withdrawals don't impact the longevity of the portfolio.

My contention is that even if we have a pot we can draw from whenever we want or need, there is merit in doing so with some regularity instead. Doing so settles the mind and provides the kind of pattern that appeals to our nature.

Rules help with decision making

There has been a great deal of scholarly work done to try to identify optimal patterns for withdrawal.

Back in Chapter 13 I mentioned Guyton and Klinger's guardrails, which provide a mechanism for deciding when and how to increase or decrease spending, depending on how well the portfolio we are relying on is performing.

Also in that chapter, I suggested that you should rely on common sense when it comes to making spending decisions. But I found that many people appreciate rules to govern those decisions.

'If-this-then-that' rules are often the most helpful in this case, for example:

> If the portfolio grows in any given year, I will increase my spending budget by 3% next year. If it falls or stays level, I will keep my spending the same.

Chapter 16: Managing Spending Patterns

This removes the need to think too hard about your spending decisions. You just set the rule and stick to it.

People don't change (much)

Remember that all the skills and discipline that got you to the point of being able to retire in the first place won't just disappear when the time comes. No one who has worked and saved hard to enjoy the last season of their life suddenly becomes a raging spendthrift when they clock off for the final time.

The steady hand on the tiller of your spending will stay rock solid as you get older.

The same is true for those who don't have good financial discipline – chances are they won't change much either.

We had a prospective client couple come to us a few years ago looking to transfer their very valuable DB pensions and convert them into DC SIPPs. He was a former bank manager and she was a former headteacher – smart, responsible people on the outside.

But they had nothing saved outside those pension schemes – no ISAs, no shares and hardly any cash set aside. It was clear to me that if we facilitated their pension transfers into a place where they could take out as much as they wanted, they would end up in penury before too long. At least with the guaranteed income from the DB schemes, they would be forced to live within that income, but with SIPPs, they'd be reduced to just the state pension in no time. We declined to work with them.

Those people were definitely the exception. In nearly every case of a retiring individual or couple I've met over the years, they continue to exercise the same good judgement in retirement as they had throughout the accumulation phase. Trust that what got you here will sustain you throughout retirement.

Everything you need to DO

Use your portfolio to provide a regular 'income'

How can you make the management of your expenditure easier in retirement?

One way is definitely to orchestrate a regular 'income' from your portfolio into your current account, This allows you to budget as you have always done.

Looking back to our example of Jane and Chris from the last chapter, Table 20 shows what they needed to have available to spend in the first couple of years.

Table 20: Chris and Jane's spending needs in years 1–2

	Risk profile	Jane pension	Jane ISA	Chris pension	Chris ISA	Bank	Total needed
Years 1–2	Risk-free	£33,520	–	£33,520	–	£22,960	£90,000

You'll remember from Table 9 in the previous chapter that we assumed £16,760 per year from each of their pension plans, made up of £4,190 tax-free cash and £12,570 income that would fall into their personal allowances. Some pension providers will allow them to take 12 'mini' UFPLS payments, which will achieve their aims while feeling very much like a regular income. The money will land in their current account at the same time every month.

Alternatively, they could arrange the full payment of the £16,760 at the beginning of the year and drop it into their savings account. From there, they could arrange a simple monthly standing order from their savings account into their current account, again making it feel like an income.

Whichever pot your money is sitting in, it's likely that you can arrange a regular withdrawal into your spending account if that's how you like to work. Regular usually means monthly but can just as easily be quarterly or half-yearly, whichever you prefer.

Decide on your own spending rules

Keep this simple and be prepared to abandon or change your rules if they don't work for you.

Let's look at a couple of examples of spending rules reviewed on an annual basis.

Example 1

At our annual review:

> If the portfolio has held steady or increased in value, we will increase our regular spending by 3% to take account of inflation.
>
> If the portfolio has fallen in value by less than 10% we will keep our spending the same for the coming year.
>
> If the portfolio has fallen in value by more than 10%, we will look at how we can reduce spending and postpone any large expenses.

Example 2

At our annual review:

> If the portfolio has increased in value, we will increase our spending by half the performance, e.g. if the portfolio has returned 8%, we will increase our spending by 4%.
>
> If the portfolio has held steady, we will maintain our spending at the same rate.
>
> If the portfolio has fallen in value, we will reduce our spending by a quarter of the performance drop, e.g. if the portfolio has returned −10% we will reduce our spending by 2.5%.

These are entirely arbitrary figures – you can pick your own or none at all.

One thing to mention is that if you do set yourself some guardrail rules like this, remember to work on the performance of the portfolio, not just its actual value.

It may be that you are planning to erode your capital, to spend it down over time. This is especially likely if you don't have children or other family that you want to benefit after you have gone.

In this case, look at how the portfolio has performed after charges and make the decision from there.

For example, if you start with £500,000, withdraw £50,000 and at the end of the year the portfolio stands at £470,000, divide the end figure into the figure after withdrawals to get a simple percentage return:

£470,000 / (£500,000 – £50,000) = 1.044, or a 4.4% return

Alternatively, you could use the tools on your investment platform to work out the actual performance of your funds and use that figure to determine your spending rule.

Don't overthink this, as I only offer it as a suggestion. As I have said (a few times now!), the fact that you are able to retire at all suggests that your spending controls are good. As long as you are prepared to adjust your spending if necessary, you will be fine.

In our discussion of the Great Transition into retirement, we've covered the Danger Zone, how to optimise cash flow for tax and convenience, how to invest to minimise sequence of returns risk and how to think about spending controls.

Pretty soon, all of this becomes second nature, and you will groove into retirement like you've always been there. The memory of working long hours recedes. You're filling your time with things that you want to do, not that you have to do.

Welcome to the New Normal.

Phase 3

The New Normal

THIS MIGHT BE THE LAST act of our lives, but there's no reason to get morbid. Think of it as the longest holiday of your life. It's the realised goal of all your efforts throughout your working life.

We should enjoy it to the full, especially in the early years. Yes, our bodies will become less reliable over time, and maybe our minds too, but while we can, this is the chance to live well, to live deeply and to make the most of every opportunity.

Chapter 17
Settling In For The Long Haul

FOR MOST OF US, RETIREMENT lasts a long time. Of course, there are always outliers – we all know someone who has died far too young – but even if we retire at state pension age, chances are there are 15–20 years of good living ahead of us, and maybe more.

So we need to make the most of it while also pacing ourselves. And yes, we are going to need to keep an eye on our finances as we go along.

Everything you need to KNOW

Spending quickly settles down

One thing I have noticed over the years is that spending in retirement peaks early on and then finds a steady level.

When we first retire, we have lots of time on our hands and hopefully the means to enjoy it. We reward ourselves with the big purchases we've been promising ourselves: the house extension, the convertible, the caravan or camper.

We may travel more in those early years too, and why shouldn't we? We've worked hard for this!

But through it all, we spend about the same each month on food and utilities. Our lifestyle costs quickly find a groove and we spend about the same on leisure activities and holidays each year. We have all the 'stuff' we need.

I think that we should embrace intelligent spending in those first few years of retirement. I'm certainly not advocating throwing all caution to the wind, but when I plan for clients, I will often model them spending more in the early retirement years than they planned.

Spending stays broadly the same through retirement, but its composition changes

There's an interesting study from the Institute of Fiscal Studies from 2022 which confirms that overall spending doesn't change that much throughout retirement.[20] The relative wealth of the household is a factor of course, but on average, spending stays within 1% in real terms of its starting point when a couple or individual retire.

What does change is the make-up of that spending. Food at home and motoring costs tend to decline as we age, but holiday spending rises until about age 80 before falling off in later life. Spending on home help like gardening and cleaning services tends to rise after age 80.

What you spend your money on is up to you, of course. I think that assuming that everyday spending will stay the same in real terms makes sense for our planning purposes. We can then look to push our spending on the 'extras' like holidays and other luxuries.

Chapter 17: Settling In For The Long Haul

Too many people spend too little, too late

I spend my life encouraging my clients to spend more, earlier. Often they are resistant to this, at least at first.

I understand why that might be the case. For the first time in decades they don't have a salary coming in, so it's natural to want to rein things in a bit. They see a finite pot of money and imagine it eroding quickly and being left dependent on a much lower income when they are older.

Good financial planning, as well as measures like the cash flow ladder we discussed earlier, can go a long way towards reassuring people that they can spend more than they think.

People don't want to waste their money. If you have managed to save enough to retire comfortably, you're very unlikely to turn into a financial profligate as soon as you turn 60.

But what are the uses of money, really? As I see it, there are three:

⇨ spending it now

⇨ investing it so that we can spend it later

⇨ giving it away.

Hoarding it till the day you die is not one of those uses. Of course, few people intentionally hoard money for its own sake. Rather, they retain money in anticipation of later life medical and care costs. As we'll see in Chapter 19, for most of us, the spectre of long-term care is never realised…

As a result, I see too many people leaving too much money on the table. They forego things in early retirement because they think they need to retain money for later life. To counter this, a key part of the planning I do for clients is modelling scenarios that show them spending more money earlier in retirement. In many cases, the clients can enjoy their early retirement to the full without compromising their later-life financial security.

Everything you need to DO

Prioritise yourself

One thing I spend a great deal of time trying to make my clients understand is that they must always prioritise themselves above everything else.

If you have children, it is understandable to have a mind to their needs, but you worked hard for *your* retirement, and you should get to enjoy it as you want to. It is rare that you'll have to make a choice between your own needs and those of your family, but if that time comes, and if you were my client, I'd be urging you to look after yourself first.

Some might call this selfish, but in truth it is almost never the case that such a decision is binary. Rather, you're likely to be able to find some outcome that balances things nicely.

It's your life and it's your money, so you must do whatever you feel comfortable doing. But I would never advocate sacrificing your own financial security to offer help to your family.

Prioritise the present

None of us has any idea how long we have on this earth. Life is not a rehearsal – we get one shot at this, and the only time we're guaranteed is now!

So while we should have a mind to the future, our priority should be living well in the present.

Again, this is about prioritisation, not binary choices. You will rarely have to choose between today and one day. Instead you may have to decide how to balance the two, and in almost every case, I would be advising you to tip the balance towards the near term because the future is not promised to us.

Retain control and plan ahead

Good financial controls are important throughout life – we should maintain some kind of a budget in retirement, even if it is very high level. We should keep an eye on our spending relative to our income and the value of our assets to ensure that we are happy with how things are going.

We must not be afraid to take a dispassionate look at our finances and address anything that we need to change as we go along.

We need to retain and refine the control over our finances that has served us so well throughout life, and a key part of that is to hold regular reviews.

So let's look at how to do that…

Chapter 18
Reviewing Your Plans

LIFE IN RETIREMENT QUICKLY SETTLES down. Sometimes it takes two or three years, but the novelty of being retired is soon replaced by settling into a nice lifestyle rhythm.

Part of that rhythm is reviewing our finances regularly to make sure everything is in a good place.

Everything you need to KNOW

Routine is a good thing

As we said in the last chapter, spending tends to settle down quickly, once the initial celebratory rewards have been enjoyed!

Life, too, settles into a familiar rhythm. Your golf/gym/beauty sessions will be on the same day each week or month. You may be looking after grandchildren or other family one day a week, or maybe having the family over for Sunday dinner once a fortnight.

We are creatures of routine – it's just the way we're built. Routine is familiar and good for the soul. While we all enjoy a change now and again, continual change is exhausting, and we find ourselves longing for a bit of normality.

As a result, there is often a kind of cyclical rhythm to financial planning. Our insurances renew annually. We might look at the value of our portfolio once a quarter, or even just when the annual statements come in. And we can lean into this steady pulse to plan in a regular review schedule.

As a general rule, our financial reviews should be annual. There really is no need to have them any more regularly than that. Remember that retirement is about living well, not micromanaging your finances! An annual review focuses the mind once a year for a couple of hours, but if done right, you can then largely leave things to run for the rest of the year, perhaps just attending to some admin if needed.

JL Collins, who wrote the book *The Simple Path To Wealth*, which I highly recommend, completes his annual financial review on his wife's birthday – I keep meaning to ask him what his wife thinks of that!

Life occasionally throws in a 5/4 bar

As a lifelong fan of the band Rush, I love the way they seamlessly change time signatures in their music. The song will keep moving forward, but there's a kind of musical skip when they drop in the odd bar of 5/4 time or similar.

While life is generally a steady routine, we all know that the universe occasionally throws us for a loop. Sometimes this is a short-term blip and then things quickly get back to normal. But sometimes these events have longer-lasting repercussions, requiring a new, different rhythm to our lives.

What might some of these blips be?

> **A health update**, especially one which might need a change of lifestyle or even shorten your life.

A relationship change for you, perhaps the loss of a partner, a relationship break-up or a new relationship with a new, long-term partner.

A family update, perhaps a new grandchild, meaning you'll be helping out your daughter more, or maybe your son is getting divorced and needs some financial help from you to get back on the housing ladder.

A financial event, perhaps an inheritance, or a significant, unexpected expense. Maybe, as happened with a client of mine recently, HMRC decides to challenge something you did over a decade ago (in this case, before they became clients!).

These events should trigger an ad hoc review of your financial planning (we'll get to how to review things in just a minute).

'Review' isn't really the right word

By definition, a review is backward looking – we are reviewing what has happened in the past. And that should be part of an annual review, but not all of it.

I have some financial planner colleagues who refuse to use the word review and come up with elaborate alternatives such as 'forward-planning meetings', but I'm going to stick with the word review for now.

The greater part of our review should be forward looking, though. Maybe just the next year or two, and maybe longer. It might be the case that the future has changed due to one of the unexpected circumstances we have just covered.

We can't change what has gone before, but we can learn from it and apply any lessons going forward. We can respond to where we find ourselves now and perhaps adjust where we see ourselves going forward from here.

A review shouldn't really focus on investment performance. Again, that's backward looking – is what it is – and if you're investing passively by tracking markets as I suggest you should, then you're just going to ride the ups and downs without making changes anyway. Continually changing your approach in light of what's already past is a recipe for hamstringing your portfolio and increasing the chances of running out of money.

Everything you need to DO

Take stock

This is the backward-looking part of the review – looking at the preceding year.

Spending

How was your spending over the past year? Did you spend more or less than you expected to? Why was that the case?

Even if you overspent compared with expectations, are you happy with that?

Do you see a pattern emerging over the past couple of years? Do you need to reset your future expectations if that pattern continues, or do you need to address the spending itself?

Investment portfolio

Don't worry too much about how the assets in your pensions and ISAs performed – that's past history. Instead, ask yourself *why* they performed as they did.

Was there a big event, like the Covid-19 pandemic or the Ukraine invasion that affected markets generally?

Did you feel like you were comfortable with how your portfolio behaved? Did you worry unduly if things were looking bleak for a while or were you indifferent? Did you understand why things happened as they did, or were you confused?

Do you think that you should adjust the risk profile of your investments, or can you leave things as they are?

Legislation changes

Big changes to financial and tax legislation happen more frequently than they should, unfortunately.

Ask yourself if any changes made will affect your planning. For example, with the reduction in the capital gains tax annual exempt allowance, does this impact your choice of whether you take money from your general investment account or your ISA?

General

Finally, think about your perspective on the year gone by. Do you feel it has been a good year, however you might define that?

Have your finances stayed largely on track, or are you in a different place from where you expected to be by now?

Looking back, would you do anything differently if those circumstances came around again? Have you learned any lessons that you feel you should keep in mind as you move forward?

By taking an objective look at the year just passed, and asking how you feel about it (which is very subjective), we can take stock in a way which hopefully leads to some useful conclusions to apply as we move forward.

Look at future income gap

We are a year further on than we were last time. We may have spent some of our cash reserves. If we built our cash flow ladder with the first two years of our spending requirements held in cash, we are halfway through that now, but we should still have at least a year of cash reserves left.

Look at your cash flow planning. Has your planned spending for the coming year changed from when you first did your plan? Is the boiler looking as if it is on its last legs; might you need to replace it soon?

Maybe the issue isn't unexpected one-off costs, but rather our general spending is higher or lower than we planned. What changes do we need to make now in light of that change?

Do we need to realise more cash for the coming year or two than we have on hand currently? Should we do this now, or if markets are distressed, should we wait a while?

Rebuild the cash flow ladder

Look back at Chapter 15 where we covered the cash flow ladder in depth.

Starting from the bottom of the ladder means looking to our short-term needs first. We need to look at the ladder as a whole, and then try to work out the shortest route from what our new ladder should look like compared with where it stands now.

If the investments higher up the ladder are looking a bit distressed, maybe just defer the review of the ladder for six months and revisit things then. Hopefully things will have improved.

If there is profit higher up, have a mind to how that money can be dropped down to top up the cash reserves. Keep in mind the tax implications of selling investments in each tax wrapper account.

In the process of reviewing your cash flow ladder, don't forget to rebalance your portfolio if things have got significantly out of balance.

If, for example, equities have a really strong year of performance, and bonds have a tough time, it's quite possible that a 60:40 portfolio could become a 70:30 or even an 80:20 portfolio.

Rebalancing is the process of selling higher-performing assets and buying lower-performing ones, to get things back in line with how you wanted to set things up. It might sound counterintuitive, but it has been proven to lead to more predictable returns if rebalancing is done intentionally.

At my planning firm, we make changes to a client's portfolio if there is a movement of more than 10% each way from our chosen allocation. So if 60:40 becomes 70:30, then we'd do a rebalance.

If you have used multi-asset funds to build your portfolio, then chances are that the funds themselves are rebalancing regularly, meaning you don't have to worry about it.

Continue to improve your situation

Even in retirement, perhaps especially so, there are a bunch of small actions which, if repeated, can make a big difference over time. Let's look at these now.

Consider making pension contributions

Even if you don't have relevant earnings, you can invest £2,880 into a pension each year and this will be increased by tax relief to £3,600 by HMRC. As I write, pensions are not included in your estate for inheritance tax calculations, so this moves money outside of the inheritance tax catch, while you still retain access.

The inheritance tax treatment is set to change from April 2027, but still, the tax relief is free money from the government – what's not to like about that?!

Use gift allowances

We're going to cover estate planning in depth in Chapter 20 but, as I write, there are generous gift allowances that enable you to give money away to family, thereby reducing your estate each year.

If you want to do this, and if you're in a position to do so, then you can plan in regular giving and improve your tax position on death on a regular basis, rather than making big gifts later on in life.

Remember that gifts to charity are exempt from inheritance tax.

Look for better interest rates

It's unlikely that you'll be able to get all your fixed-term deposit maturities synced with your annual review date, so this is likely to happen throughout the year. But it's obviously worth your time to look around for the best interest rates you can on your money.

Don't obsess about this. If the difference between your well-known high street bank and some obscure online-only offering you've never heard of is only 0.05%, then I'd probably stick with the recognisable name.

Make sure that any bank you're considering is covered by the Financial Services Compensation Scheme and has a UK banking licence.

There are schemes available now where you invest your money and the service will look for the best rates for you while also keeping large deposits split over several banks to keep each deposit within the FSCS limits. Essentially they shop around for you, which can be a great time saver. Two notable providers are HL Active Cash and Raisin, but others are available, so do your own research.

Look for better prices on utilities and other regular costs

It is easier than ever to shop around for lower prices thanks to comparison sites.

Don't accept the renewal costs of your house or car insurance at face value. Shop around and see how much you can save – the differences are often huge!

Same goes for your mobile phone contract, your TV package and your utilities. Every pound you're spending on these things is a pound you can't enjoy on living well, so demand value at every point.

Chapter 18: Reviewing Your Plans

The great thing about comparison sites is that your searches are saved, so each year it gets easier as you only need to make small tweaks to get the most up-to-date prices. Usually you can get the latest search results in under five minutes.

Reviewing your finances in retirement is really about making sure the right money is in the right place at the right time. All the detail above leads to this outcome.

After that, retirement is about living well. Don't let your finances dominate your life. You can review everything I set out above in a couple of hours once a year. That leaves lots of hours left to have fun!

Chapter 19
Later Life Planning

MOST OF US WILL HAVE a decent length of time to enjoy our retirement. Time marches on inexorably though, and inevitably we grow older and start to think about what happens in later life and even once we are no longer around.

In this chapter I want to help you plan for the challenges of later life and in Chapter 20, we'll look at things like estate planning, pension death benefits and trusts.

Everything you need to KNOW

Losing a partner is a big deal

The bulk of this book is about the transition into retirement, which is clearly one of the most profound financial changes any of us make in our lives. But when it comes to considering the biggest overall shock to our system, financial, psychological and emotional, I don't think they get any bigger than the loss of a life partner.

I'm not the right person to go into the personal trauma of losing someone who has been part of your life for decades. But time and time again, I have seen the financial impact on my clients and yet, in many cases, the financial trauma could have been minimised, if not removed altogether.

In many partnerships, one partner is 'the one who does the money'. They are the ones who handle insurance renewals, know what the bills come to and have the logins to the electricity and broadband accounts. Every partnership is different, of course, and some are very much a team effort.

The most dysfunctional financial partnership I ever saw was where the lady of the couple handled everything. And I mean everything – the chap didn't even know the PIN for his own bank card. She used to give him pocket money each week to go and play snooker with his mates.

All was well until she experienced rapid-onset vascular dementia. Within a fortnight, she was incapable of handling anything and he was financially bereft, on top of the trauma of seeing his wife become a shell of her former self.

The financial demands of life don't stop when one of us dies or loses capacity. Those bills still need to be paid, and while most institutions will show some forbearance in a difficult situation, before too long things need to be dealt with.

We know that death is inevitable. We may retain full physical and mental capacity till the end, but we may not. But while we are in full control of our faculties, we must prepare for the worst.

Long-term care is not the spectre many think it is

The majority of my clients are aged over 60 years old – that's the nature of my work. And I don't think a week has passed since I started this career that someone hasn't mentioned long-term care to me.

In many societies in the world, it is the responsibility and duty of the younger generations of a family to look after the elders. Here in the West, this is less the case these days and a whole industry and bureaucratic system has arisen to meet the needs of the senior members of our society. Our bodies and minds fail, and when they do, we're going to need some kind of help with day-to-day living, personal care and medical intervention.

The Alzheimer's Society report in 2024 states that 982,000 people in the UK are living with some form of dementia. This is projected to rise to 1.4 million people by 2040.

According to the 2021 census, there were over 11 million people aged 65 and over living in England and Wales. Only 4% of this cohort were living in care homes.

Of those aged over 85, 15% were in full-time residential care – this includes both residential and nursing homes.

According to Age UK, the average weekly cost of a care home in the UK is £800 (£41,600 per year), and for a nursing home, you're looking at an average of £1,078 per week (£56,056 per year).

If you need long-term care, your local authority will conduct a financial assessment to see how much they have to contribute towards the cost of your care. If you have assets, including the value of your property, of more than £23,250 (in the 2024/25 tax year) then you're going to be paying for all of your care costs. Below that the local authority will subsidise the cost and once your assets drop below £14,250, they will bear all the cost.

All of your income will need to be used to pay for your care, minus a small personal expenses allowance which rises by inflation each year and goes to pay for haircuts, hygiene products and the like. Of course, if you are financially supporting a spouse who is not in care, then this is factored into the financial assessment.

You can understand why older folks would be concerned about the impact of those sorts of costs on their finances and on the legacy they would like to leave to their family.

But let's think this through.

The ONS average life expectancy at age 85 is 3.6 years for females and 2.6 years for males. Obviously many will live shorter or longer lives than that – that's how averages work!

A 15% chance of needing care at age 85 equates to a one in six-and-a-half chance of that being you. And if you do need care, it probably won't be for that long.

So given that nearly every couple in their 70s that I speak to mention their worries about needing care, is this actually a disproportionate fear?

I can think of only two clients in the more than 25 years I've been doing my job who have had their entire estates wiped out by care fees. For each one of those there have probably been 500 couples who have had all their needs met, including care in later life, and have still been able to leave a meaningful legacy to their family.

I don't mean to belittle the impact of care costs, but I do think that too many people leave too much money on the table, because they worry about something that never happens to them.

You can eat your house

When you've done a job as long as I have, you inevitably end up coining some daft but useful phrases that get trotted out regularly when speaking with clients. One such gem is 'you can't eat your house', by which I mean that a house is first and foremost a home, and if you do need to sell it, it's not as easy as taking money out of an ISA or a pension, say. The value of a home is locked up in the bricks and mortar.

But it's not strictly true to say that you can't eat your house anymore because there is a mechanism by which you can take value out of your property and have it available to spend on your daily needs. This mechanism is called Equity Release.

There are three ways you can release the value of your home: downsize your property, arrange a lifetime mortgage or arrange a home reversion plan.

Downsizing is where you sell your place and buy something for a lower price, with the difference being banked and available for you to spend. There are always costs involved in moving, of course, from estate agents and legal fees to the stamp duty on the new place. There is no personal tax involved in selling your primary residence, though.

Another option is a *lifetime mortgage*. Now there's nothing more likely to make retired folks wince than the word 'mortgage'. After all, you worked hard to pay off your mortgage and now, no one can kick you out of your home.

But a lifetime mortgage isn't like an ordinary mortgage. You can arrange it so that there are no monthly payments to make; instead the debt rolls up over time. Interest rates are usually fixed or capped so you can know exactly how much you will owe at any point in the future. There are versions of the lifetime mortgage that act like a facility from which you can draw only as you need to, like a big overdraft, essentially. You only pay interest on the amount that you have drawn down.

These kinds of arrangements used to be the wild west of financial services, completely unregulated. You may have heard horror stories of families losing their loved ones only to be left owing more than the family home was worth.

Thankfully, there are now very stringent protections for people taking out these kinds of mortgages. The Equity Release Council has a set of voluntary standards that all good Equity Release firms adhere to. Things like a no-negative equity guarantee, so you can never owe more than the house is worth; the right to remain in your property for life or until you need full-time, permanent residential care; and the right to port the mortgage to another property, so you can move home, as long as the new property is mortgageable.

You should make sure any lifetime mortgage you apply for meets these standards to the letter.

Most people who consider taking out a lifetime mortgage are

concerned about the value of their home being eroded completely by the debt, but in practice this is unlikely.

In Figure 7, I use an example of a 70-year-old couple borrowing £100,000 on a property worth £350,000. You can see how much the debt (the darker line) rolls up – I have used a 5% interest rate as an example. You can also see that the property also increases in value (the lighter line), and I've only used a 1% property growth rate here.

Figure 7: Example of roll-up of debt vs value of property

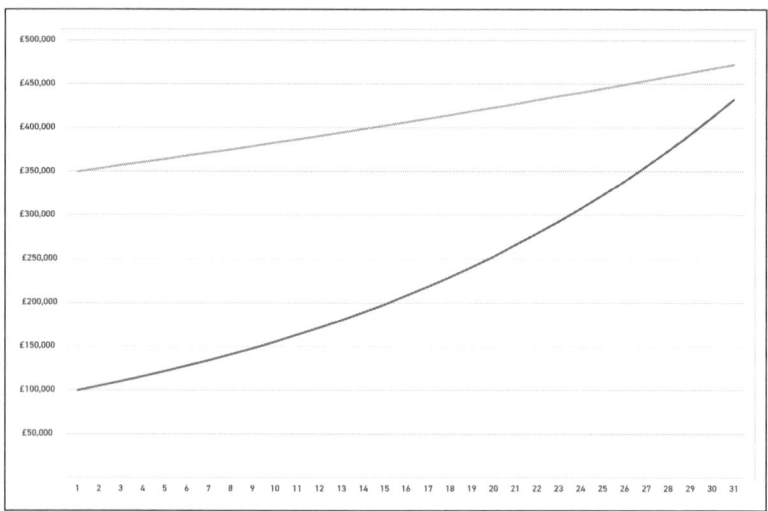

Clearly, if the debt rolls up at a higher interest rate and/or the property doesn't grow in value, you could end up with the two lines meeting, and the value of the property being matched by the debt owed. In the figure above, however, there is still plenty of equity in the house as time goes on, as follows:

At age 80, there is £223,728 equity

At age 90, there is £161,736 equity

And at age 100, there is still £39,552 equity available in the property.

If I keep the mortgage interest rate the same, but increase the property annual growth to just 2%, there is still £201,782 of equity left in the property at age 100.

This is why the lenders of lifetime mortgages put limits on how much you can borrow, based on your age. The younger you are, the longer the debt has to roll up, and so the less they will lend you at the outset.

It may be the case that you can make further arrangements with your lifetime mortgage company to borrow more in later years. If you have arranged a facility with a lender, the interest rate on future tranches will be set at the time you take that money.

One thing to bear in mind is that these mortgages are designed never to be paid off. The early redemption penalties can be quite steep, up to 25% of the amount owed. These do not apply if you die or go into full-time, permanent residential care. But if you win the lottery and decide you don't want the mortgage anymore, paying it off can be expensive. Then again, if you have won the lottery, you probably don't care!

These are now mature products which are ideal for the right people at the right time. So much so in fact, that I arranged one for my own parents.

The third and final method for releasing equity from your property is called a *home reversion plan*. Here, you sell your property to the home reversion company, for much less than it is worth, in return for a tax-free lump sum.

You still have the right to stay in your property until you die or need long-term care, but there is no option to borrow more in the future.

There is no interest rolling up either, though, so it removes the complexity for your family of having to sell a mortgaged property when you have gone.

I have yet to come across a case where a home reversion makes more sense than a lifetime mortgage. And I've yet to find a client who is happy with the idea of selling their home for less than it is worth.

Lifetime mortgages and home reversion plans should be considered a last resort, only to be used if there is no other way of releasing the money you need. I always encourage clients considering these options to discuss things with their family before they commit, as the family will inevitably be affected by the choice to take out one of these plans.

It makes no sense to die rich

The last thing I want to cover in this extended KNOW section is my belief that dying rich is an odd choice, when the alternative is to live more fully than you might have.

Look, everyone has their own definition of what it means to live well – maybe your definition means that you won't get anywhere close to spending all your money; that's your choice.

The other problem is that we don't know the day we're going to die, which makes it tricky to plan on spending our last pound that morning!

We pay tax all our working lives, when we buy property and other assets, and when we sell them, in some cases. We pay VAT on our day-to-day needs. And then – the final insult – we may pay inheritance tax when we die, too.

I'm going to cover estate planning in the next chapter, but suffice it to say that I'd rather more of my estate gets enjoyed by my family than by HMRC, after I've gone. Going further, I'd rather my estate is enjoyed firstly by me, and then by my family *while I'm still alive*, than by HMRC when I die.

Some people call inheritance tax the voluntary tax because it can be planned around, given enough time and clear intent. We'll look at how to do that shortly.

Please remember – your money is your money. You earned it, saved it and invested it – you and your loved ones should be the ones who benefit, so please don't leave estate planning to chance. And consider spending more than you are.

Everything you need to DO

Make or review your wills

If you haven't made a will yet, stop reading at the end of this section and find someone to do it for you. Likewise, if you haven't updated your will in a while, then now would be a good time to do so. A will writer or a full solicitor – either will serve; just don't try and write it yourself. And please don't use a DIY will kit from WH Smiths. While you *can* write a will yourself, I've seen that go wrong enough times for me never to recommend it as an option.

Your will is simply a record of your instructions for what you want to happen to your stuff when you die. You appoint some people to sort it all out for you, called executors, and then tell them what you want to happen when the time comes.

Their job is firstly to add up the value of everything at the date of your death. If there are any debts, those are taken off the value. These figures are submitted to HMRC to see if there is any inheritance tax payable. If there is, then the tax must be paid first, before anything is distributed to the beneficiaries. Once the tax is paid, or it is determined that no tax is due, then a Grant of Probate is issued which is the authorisation from the government to your executors that they can go ahead and start paying out to those named in your will. If the deceased person only has a small amount of money (less than about £10,000) in their name and no property, probate may not be needed.

There is a reason why wills are written in the language that they are. Centuries of legal precedent have set the meaning of various words and phrases to be as unambiguous as possible. You want your wishes to be clear, and whoever writes your will, it's their job to translate your wishes into clear language.

Anyone can challenge a will after you have died. They are a matter of public record if probate is required, but only once it is granted. Before that, the only people with a right to see the will are the executors. Not even the beneficiaries have a right to do so.

If you die without a will, you are said to have died 'intestate'. In this case your estate will be distributed according to the laws of intestacy, which may or may not reflect your wishes. By making a will, you are removing this chance and making sure what you want to happen, does happen.

If you haven't made a will already, sit down (together if you are in a couple) and think and talk about what your wishes might be. This can be challenging, especially if there are children from previous marriages to consider.

Think about the people you would want to benefit. Also, are there any causes that are close to your heart, like your local church, a local sports club or a particular charity perhaps (a popular one down here in Cornwall is the RNLI)?

The order of operations in a will is usually that you make specific bequests (gifts) first, for example:

> 'I would like my neighbour Joe Bloggs to have £10,000 because he has helped me with my shopping every week for years.'
>
> 'I would like to give each of my grandchildren £10,000.'
>
> 'I give the 24ct gold diamond solitaire ring, that I inherited from my mother, to my daughter Sarah.'

After the specific gifts, the residuary estate is divided up, usually in percentages. So you might say that everything should be sold and divided equally between your three children, for example.

Try not to think about what the beneficiaries might think of you as you are planning this. Remember that this is *your* property to do with as you like; you shouldn't put yourself under any pressure as to where it all ends up. And certainly no one else, even your spouse or partner, should be putting you under any pressure – you must resist that at all costs.

When you have decided what you want to happen, that's the point at which you should talk to a professional who will write down those wishes for you. They will also point out any issues that might arise and suggest workarounds or alternatives to you.

Please, don't delay making a will. Dying intestate can cause huge delays and extra costs in sorting everything out, adding to the burden on your loved ones at an already difficult time.

Ensure you have Lasting Powers of Attorney in place

Though none of us like to think of it, there may come a time when we no longer have the capacity to manage our own affairs. This may be due to a sudden medical event such as a stroke or a gradual one such as the onset of dementia. It may just be that eventually we get tired of life admin and want to hand it over to someone we trust (our attorney) to do this on our behalf. For that, we need a Lasting Power of Attorney (LPA).

There are two types of LPA. The first is a *property and financial* LPA where you give control over your investments, bank accounts, insurances, pensions and property to your attorneys. It is possible for you to trigger your property and financial LPA intentionally, even while you still have your faculties.

The second type is the *health and welfare* LPA, which allows your chosen attorneys to make decisions regarding medical treatment, long-term care and even end-of-life care. This one can only come into effect when you lose capacity to make those decisions for yourself. Your loss of capacity would have to be confirmed by medical professionals, which gives you protection from being declared incapable by unscrupulous family members.

Your chosen attorneys are bound by very strict rules over what they can and can't do in your name. They can continue making gifts on your behalf to family for Christmas and birthdays, for example, but they are not allowed to make gifts outside of that structure.

You can have an LPA made up by a solicitor, but unlike a will, this is very easy to do yourself. The gov.uk website makes it very easy. You just need to know the names and addresses of:

⇨ you, the *donor*

⇨ your chosen *attorneys*

⇨ your *certificate provider*, someone who knows you and can certify that you understand the implications of entering into an LPA and that you are not under duress as you do so.

You will also need a witness who is unconnected to you to be present when the document is signed.

Once everything is signed, the forms are sent off to the Office of the Public Guardian to be registered. This usually takes three or four months and at the time of writing costs £82 per LPA, unless you get special dispensation if you are on a low income, in which case the fee is halved to £41 per LPA.

If you lose capacity to manage your affairs without an LPA in place then, again, this makes life very difficult for your family. Don't think that your next of kin can automatically just take over everything. An LPA gives them authority to do so, but in the absence of that, they must apply to the Office of the Public Guardian who will choose someone to be a 'deputy'. This can take months and is a more expensive process than applying for an LPA.

Please don't put this off. Having both a will and LPAs in place is a big tick on your to-do list and will be a great weight off your mind.

Stay healthy

I presume that most of us want to live as long as possible; I know I do. But that sentiment sometimes changes as we get older. Plenty of people have told me that they just want to call it a day, especially when they get ill or feel like they are becoming a burden on their loved ones.

As a financial planner, I usually plan for every client to reach age 100. When I tell them this, their response is often 'oh, I hope I don't live that long!'

Our health is a combination of genetics and our choices. Past choices are just that – in the past – and there's nothing we can do to change them. But we can seek to make better choices for our health going forward, with the intention of living as well as we can for as long as we can.

Two excellent books on living well are *How Not To Die* by Dr Michael Greger, which includes chapters such as 'How not to die of dementia'; and *The Retirement Café Handbook* by Justin King, who is a financial planner. His podcast of the same name is worth a listen, too.

Prepare for the loss of a partner

As morbid as it sounds, we need to spend some time thinking about the implications of losing our partner.

If you are the one who holds the financial reins, then I think the onus is on you to make sure that if you go first, the one left behind has everything they need to pick up where you left off.

So make a list of financial accounts, insurance policies, direct debits and other bills, pensions and other incomes. Basically everything that goes in or out of your bank account needs to be written down, including account numbers where possible. Include contact details of the providers, too, so that your partner isn't scratching around looking for that information when the time comes. Be careful when writing down login information, and make sure it is stored securely, but that your partner knows where.

Take some time to think about what the financial situation would be when one of you dies. What would happen to your pension income? What happens to your state pension? What income is your partner going to be left with? What bills will stop?

Make sure that plenty of money is held jointly or that they have enough in their own name, because if you die suddenly, they need to have access to enough money to get them through a few months while everything is sorted out.

If you are the financially passive one, then make sure your partner is getting this information together.

I have seen the chaos that being unprepared for death can cause. The emotional and psychological impact of losing your life partner is challenging enough, but adding financial pressure to that is horrific, especially as it is avoidable.

Don't shy away from difficult conversations. Take the bull by the horns and put these things in place – it's a great legacy and example to set for your family.

Chapter 20
Estate Planning

AS RETIREMENT CONTINUES, BEFORE TOO long many people get to the point where they have everything they need, they are content with their lifestyle and they start to think about passing money and assets down the generations to their family.

Often the motivation for this is inheritance tax, as we mentioned in the last chapter, but a better motivation is to see your estate in the right hands and, ideally, even before you have passed away!

Everything you need to KNOW

How inheritance tax works

There has been some kind of tax payable on death since the late 17th century, but its form has changed throughout the years since.

Needless to say, inheritance tax (IHT) is wildly unpopular. It feels like the last insult after a lifetime of paying tax in various forms. It doesn't contribute very much to the Exchequer, but the pounds and pence figure is rising. In 2023/24, IHT revenues were about £7.3 billion, up from £6.1 billion two years prior to that.[21] The expected budget in 2024/25 is £1.226 trillion with IHT expected to be £7.6 billion, just 0.6% of the total budget.

I rarely hear people complain about VAT, or even income tax, but IHT is a frequent topic of heated discussion in my client conversations!

The value of your estate is basically everything you own in your own name, plus half of what you own in joint names with your spouse or legal partner, minus everything you owe.

At the time of writing, everyone gets two main allowances on death:

> **The Nil Rate Band.** This is currently £325,000, meaning that amount of your estate is free of IHT.
>
> **The Residence Nil Rate Band (RNRB).** This is a further £175,000 of tax-free allowance, which applies if you leave your primary residence – or the proceeds of its sale – to your 'direct descendants'. Note that if you have no direct descendants, you don't get an RNRB, which hardly seems fair. Also, if the value of your home is less than the RNRB, the remaining allowance can't be used to offset against other assets.

Add those two together and you get an inheritance tax-free allowance of £500,000 each. As there is never any IHT to pay when passing assets between spouses, if the nil rate bands remain unused on the death of the first partner, they can be passed to the survivor for use on their death, making a potential £1 million of IHT-free estate that can be passed down to the next generation.

The value of your estate above the nil rate bands is subject to inheritance tax at 40%.

Unsurprisingly, it isn't quite as simple as that – there are wrinkles to the rules that keep me and your local solicitor in a job.

For example, the RNRB is progressively removed if your estate is over £2 million. Over £2.35 million and the RNRB is removed altogether.

Also, that £2m threshold is on the date of death. We have advised people to make gifts to family in their dying weeks and months to bring their estate below that threshold. Those gifts will fall foul of the seven-year rule (more on this below), but they do bring the estate value down immediately, preserving the RNRB.

There are four main ways you can mitigate inheritance tax while you are alive. Let's look at each in turn.

1. Spend your money

If it's not there when you die because you've blown it all on great holidays and good living, it can't be taxed!

In practice many people find this difficult, as I mentioned previously in this book. Our habits don't change just because we're getting older. We likely have all the stuff we need and conspicuous consumption, even for the purposes of tax reduction, seems daft.

Making small changes like upgrading from Economy Plus to Business or even First Class when going on holiday is one way to spend more without it feeling like a waste.

2. Give your money away

If we feel uncomfortable spending money on ourselves, helping our family often feels much better. In fact, I'd say that giving, whether to family, friends or to causes that we care about, is the highest calling for the wealth that we have built. We should feather our own nest first, of course, and make sure all our own needs are met, but after that, there is real joy in giving generously.

There are rules that preclude making death-bed gifts to reduce your IHT bill, but intentional giving over time is a very effective tax planning solution. Note that gifts to charities are always tax free whether made in life or through your will. Giving 10% or more of your estate to charity has the effect of reducing your IHT rate on the balance to 36%.

In order to prevent death-bed giving, the *seven-year rule* applies to lifetime gifts. This states that if you die within seven years of making a gift, then the tax on that gift is payable on a sliding scale. The full tax at 40% is payable if you die within three years of making the gift. The rate is 32% if you die in year four, 24% in year five, 16% in year six, 8% in year seven and then no tax if you die after a full seven years has passed since the date of the gift. This only applies if the value of your estate including the gift is above the nil rate band when you die.

There are some gift exemptions which mean that you can make gifts and have them immediately outside your estate for inheritance tax purposes. These are:

Annual gift exemption. Each person can give a gift of up to £3,000 each tax year. If you didn't use the exemption last year, you can go back one year.

Small gifts. You can give as many small gifts of £250 to as many different people as you like.

Wedding or civil partnership. On the occasion of a wedding, parents can give a child a £5,000 gift with no IHT implications. Grandparents and great-grandparents can give £2,500 and anyone else can give £1,000.

Gifts from income. Gifts which are made out of disposable income (not capital) are immediately exempt from IHT as long as they are regular and do not reduce the donor's standard of living.

Gifts to charities and political parties. Any lifetime gifts made to charities or political parties are exempt from inheritance tax.

3. Insure the tax liability

You can take out a whole-of-life insurance policy with a death benefit set to something like the amount of your IHT bill. This doesn't reduce the bill, of course, it just provides a way for it to be paid. In essence, you're paying the bill on a monthly instalment basis while you're alive. Of course, the quicker you die, the fewer premiums you will pay to the insurer, and the better off your estate will be, but I don't think an early demise is something to aim for!

Life insurance is expensive at older ages, and it's likely that there may be some medical issues that will increase your premiums and even preclude you from getting cover altogether. The only way to know is to apply though. I always recommend that people use the brilliant team at LifeSearch for their life insurance needs. Head to meaningfulmoney.tv/lifesearch and they will advise you about what kind of policy is best for your circumstances. A financial planner can also assist you with this if needed.

You should always place life insurance in a trust. Otherwise, the benefits will be paid *into* your estate and make your IHT position even worse. The trust ring-fences the money when it pays out, and makes it available to your executors quickly, so they can pay the IHT bill when it becomes due.

If you are in a couple, you could consider a joint life, second death policy, which may end up being a slightly cheaper option.

Make sure to understand whether your premiums are fixed or whether they increase throughout life. If fixed, they will likely start much higher.

You could also think about using your investments to produce an income to pay for the life insurance premiums.

4. Business relief

As I write, business relief (BR) – sometimes still called by its old name, business property relief or BPR – is a powerful tool for reducing your IHT liability. It exists to protect family businesses from having to be sold to pay IHT, but its rules can be applied to other kinds of investments.

In the Autumn Budget 2024, the Government announced changes to the business relief regime to come into force from April 2026.

If you own a business in whole or in part, then it will likely qualify for BR. I own 50% of the shares in my company. When I die, the value of those shares will not be counted in an IHT calculation.

But after April 2026, just the first £1 million worth of shares will be excluded from IHT; any value over that amount will be taxable, but with a 50% relief. So inheritance tax would be payable at 20%, not 40%, on the excess value over £1 million.

Shares in unlisted companies including, perhaps confusingly, those shares listed on the AIM stock market may also qualify, though things are set to change from April 2026. Here, there is no £1 million allowance – the full value of the AIM-listed shares will be chargeable to inheritance tax, but with a 50% relief.

Shares in listed companies do not qualify, so if you have some old BT or Vodafone shares, you're out of luck.

There are two other criteria for shares to qualify – the company must be a trading company, that is, it must exist for the purposes of carrying on a trade of some kind, whether that's plumbing, selling cars or financial advice. And you must have held the shares for at least two years and still hold them at the date of death.

Unsurprisingly, investment companies have contrived ways for you to benefit from business relief using off-the-shelf investments. You invest in the shares of a single, unlisted company, which will do some kind of trade so that it qualifies. I have seen companies engaged in first-charge mortgage lending, renewable energy and even ticket sales for major events.

Often these plans are marketed as low risk, but you're investing in the shares of a single, unlisted company. By definition, that's a high-risk play and it's possible that if the company fails, you could lose everything.

Far better, I think, to invest in AIM-listed shares, which you can do yourself, or there are investment managers who will build AIM portfolios for you. At least you know that these are fairly liquid – you can get your money out – even if they are still a high-risk proposition.

It's worth mentioning here that farming businesses may qualify for a similar relief called Agricultural Property Relief, or APR. This is also set to change from April 2026. Chances are that if you qualify for this, you're already working with an accountant who can help you navigate it, so I won't cover this any further here.

So, four options for reducing your IHT, so stay tuned until the DO section for some practical suggestions.

How pension death benefits work

If you recall, back in Chapters 7 and 8 we discussed the two major types of pension in the UK: DB and DC schemes.

DB schemes pay you a guaranteed income in retirement. Usually there is a spouse's benefit built in, so that if you, the pensioner, die first, then your legal partner will receive a guaranteed income for the rest of their life, albeit reduced from the level you enjoy. Usually the spouse will receive half or two-thirds of the full pension.

DC schemes, you will remember, are in the form of a fund which is built up throughout your working life until at some point in the future, you must decide what to do with it.

If you used your pension fund to buy an annuity when you retired, then the death benefits will depend on the options you chose. Again, there may be a spouse's benefit if you chose one, or there may be the balance of a guaranteed minimum payment period which will usually pay into your estate.

If you opted for drawdown or UFPLS payments instead and you still have a pension fund that you haven't fully used, then, as I write, the balance of that fund is held in a kind of master trust arrangement and sits outside of your estate. That means it is not subject to the terms of your will.

Instead, you will have completed an *expression of wishes* form when you took out the pension. Be sure to check this is in place and make sure it still reflects your wishes.

The pension company acts as trustee on the death benefits. Your expression of wishes form is there to guide them as to who you would like the money paying to, but doesn't bind the trustees.

Some forms will ask you to choose a percentage that you would like to go to each person, but you don't have to complete this. It is a good idea to put down anyone on the form that you might want to benefit, because then they are known to the trustees and are in contention to receive money when the time comes.

I have seen cases where because the adult children weren't named on the form, they were either overlooked completely or were limited as to the form their benefits could take. In larger estates particularly, we always make sure that the children are mentioned at the very least. Often the widow(er) has other assets from which they can draw, so we arrange for the pension to miss them out and drop to the children.

In her Autumn Budget 2024, Rachel Reeves revealed that pensions will be brought back into the IHT regime from April 2027. As we go to press, this is still under consultation, so we don't yet know what the full rules will be, but on the surface, it looks like all unused pension funds will potentially be subject to inheritance tax at 40%.

How pensions work on death depends on whether you die before age 75 or after:

> **Before age 75.** If you sadly die before you reach your 75th birthday, then, as I write, your fund will pass to your beneficiaries. Either they can receive a lump sum into their bank (tax free up to £1,073,100), or they can retain it as a pension fund, called a dependant's or successor's drawdown, from which they can draw tax free for life, even if they themselves haven't reached the normal minimum pension age.
>
> **After age 75.** If you die after your 75th birthday, the fund will still pass to your beneficiaries without any tax on the transfer, but they will pay income tax on anything they draw out of the fund. If they take it as a lump sum, they will pay income tax on

the lot. Most people opt for a drawdown plan so they can plan to take withdrawals as tax efficiently as possible.

If you know how your pension will work if you die first, you can plan for the inevitable day when your time comes.

If one partner has the lion's share of the pension, particularly if it's a DB scheme, then you should definitely think about what might happen if you die early, and your partner has to live a long time with only half of your pension, perhaps.

If it's a DC scheme, then chances are your remaining fund will pass to your spouse and they can carry on drawing from it as you were.

But don't leave anything to chance. Think through some scenarios and plan accordingly.

How trusts work, and why you probably don't need one

Lots of clients ask me about trusts and in 99% of cases I manage to put them off the idea. Trusts are complex and expensive to run, in many cases, and they are certainly not to be entered into lightly.

Think of a trust as a box. In that box is the trust property, whatever thing you put in there to protect and ring-fence it.

Because you set up the trust, you are called the *settlor*. You will automatically be a *trustee*, but you should also appoint further trustees – it is their job to look after the box and follow the instructions in the *trust deed* (the document that creates the trust). Finally, you have the *beneficiaries*, those who will benefit from whatever is in the box whenever you have determined that they should do so.

In the trust deed are instructions about who gets what and when, and what happens to the trust property in the meantime. Also governing this are some laws specific to trusts and how they are treated. The trust deed can either be a stand-alone document, or you can write a trust as part of your will.

Trusts fall into two main types:

Bare or absolute trusts where the beneficiaries are named.

Discretionary trusts, where the beneficiaries may be described by class, such as 'my children, grandchildren and remoter issue' and the trustees have discretion as to how such individuals may benefit.

You might use a bare trust if you want to leave money to a minor grandchild in your will. When you die, the money will go into the trust and when they reach the age you specify, they will receive the proceeds.

A discretionary trust is usually used when you want to keep your options open, or if you want to prevent money being counted in your beneficiary's estate. So if you want to give some money to help your disabled adult child, but don't want them to lose their state benefits, setting up a discretionary trust which potentially benefits all your children means that your disabled child has no absolute right to that money, and hence their benefits should remain intact.

As you can imagine, this is a complex area, and we haven't even looked at how trusts are taxed. For this reason, you should tread very carefully with trusts. They are complex and can be costly to run both in terms of money and time.

Definitely seek legal advice from a qualified and experienced solicitor.

However, you probably don't need to use trusts in your estate planning. It is almost always a better idea to give the money to the beneficiary directly. There are no immediate tax implications, you don't need a lawyer and it's quick and easy.

Using a trust instead can incur immediate IHT (yes, even while you're alive) in some circumstances. The trust will need to be registered with the government. You will possibly have to complete a tax return. The money in the trust should be invested, which also comes at a cost, and if you get the investments wrong, could lead to legal action being taken against you by the beneficiaries.

I think that most people should stay well clear of trusts unless they have a very large estate or they have relatives with issues like disabilities or addiction which might make ring-fencing the money preferable.

There's one more point I want to make around trusts. You may see companies offering to protect the value of your home against long-term care costs by using something called a Family Protection Trust. The idea is that you transfer your home into trust so that it isn't technically yours anymore. When the local authority does their financial assessment around paying for care, the property doesn't factor and is preserved for your family.

Please, avoid these things like the plague. Why anyone would want to give up ownership of their home is beyond me. In addition, it's likely that the local authority might just decide to set aside the trust and treat you as if you still owned the property.

If you're in a position where your only asset is your house, and you set up a Family Protection Trust, you don't own it anymore. Yes, the local authority may end up paying for your care, but that means you're at their mercy when it comes to which home you're in and where it is situated.

I understand wanting to leave a legacy for your children, but you should prioritise yourself, remember. If you die with nothing left, then so be it. At least you will have spent everything you have on your own comfort in your final years.

Everything you need to DO

Calculate your inheritance tax

The first step in taking action with estate planning is to add up your estate and calculate your IHT liability.

There are many online calculators that will help you do this, but one of the simplest is on the Hargreaves Lansdown website.[22]

To complete the calculation you will need to have the following information to hand:

⇨ the value of your main residence

⇨ the value of any other property(ies)

⇨ the value of your savings and investments

⇨ how much life cover will pay out (assuming it is not in trust)

⇨ the combined value of your other possessions, the contents of your home, your cars, etc.

⇨ the value of any trusts of which you are a life tenant (this usually means that you get the income from the trust but can't access the capital)

⇨ the balance of what you owe on:

- your mortgage
- credit cards
- loans
- overdrafts

⇨ how much you have given away in gifts over the last seven years.

This will give you an idea of the extent of your IHT liability and whether it's a problem or not. Sometimes it comes as a shock to people when we calculate their liability for the first time, and it usually galvanises them into taking action.

If you multiply the tax liability by 2.5 you have an idea of how much you need to reduce the value of your estate by in order to remove the problem.

By way of example, let's say you work out that your IHT liability is £60,000. Multiplying that by 2.5 means that you would have to reduce the size of your estate by £150,000 to eliminate your IHT liability. Keep this figure in mind.

Chapter 20: Estate Planning

Calculate a basic lifetime capital requirement

It is useful to have some idea of the amount of capital you're likely to need for the rest of your life. Here is a very simplified method for doing that.

Once you have reached state pension age and all your likely sources of income are paying out to you, you will have a total income figure that's easy to work out. Use the after-tax figure. Let's say that's £40,000.

Now think about your average annual costs. You might need to look back at a few years and come up with an average so that you account for both higher and lower years. Maybe one year you don't take a holiday and in another year you change the car. Let's say the average annual spend is £50,000. That means you are drawing down off your capital by an average of £10,000 each year.

Multiply that figure by the number of years you have left to live. Oh wait, we don't know that timescale, so we'll have to guess! Use age 100 as a guide because you just never know. If you're age 70 now, then multiply the £10,000 by 30 years to get £300,000.

We're assuming that your expenses will rise by inflation but we're also going to assume that your capital will increase at a rate higher than inflation, which it should if it is well invested. That means that we can use our figure of £300,000 as the amount of capital we want to keep on hand to meet our future needs.

By planning to age 100 we are probably being conservative. If we want to err even more on the side of caution, perhaps to factor in long-term care costs, you could multiply your capital figure by 1.5, say, to get £450,000.

That's the amount of invested capital we want to retain access to. If our assumptions are borne out, we can consider giving away the excess over that figure.

Let's say our invested capital, excluding the value of our home, is £750,000, and we only need £450,000 to cover our costs for the rest of our lives. We could now consider making gifts sooner rather than later out of the £300,000 difference.

Remember how we calculated that we needed to reduce our estate by £150,000 to eliminate IHT? Well, that is now looking very affordable.

Start giving

I do not expect you just to start writing big cheques to your children on the basis of what is a very simplistic calculation. But you can make a start.

At the very least, begin using your annual gift exemptions and your small gifts exemptions, but consider getting a head start with a larger gift. Pick a figure you're comfortable with, and make the gift.

You will feel great when it is done. The recipient will be delighted, of course, and hopefully very grateful. You will have made a difference to your IHT bill and seen your family enjoy the benefit of your gift, or seen the difference your favourite charity can make with the money.

Giving becomes addictive. Once you start, you will get a feel for it and will enjoy the pleasure that giving can bring you.

Always do so intentionally. Redo the calculation once a year at your annual review and think about where your gifts can have the biggest benefit.

Keep good records of gifts made. Keep a dedicated spreadsheet for the purpose or even just a notebook. All you need to do is note three pieces of information:

⇨ date of the gift

⇨ recipient

⇨ amount.

You may also want to keep proof in the form of a receipt from the person or charity you have given the money to. Bank statements showing the amounts going out will also serve. Keep these records somewhere, perhaps with your will, and let your executors know where they are.

Seek professional advice

I spend the majority of my time as a financial planner working on one of two issues for my clients – the transition into retirement and estate planning. For long-standing clients, I've worked through both life stages.

There's no doubt that this is where we add the most value to our clients' lives. In some cases, with one simple form, I have saved a client hundreds of thousands of pounds. Recently I moved two pensions for a client couple. Because they were old pensions, if they had been left where they were, there would have been a tax charge of about £600,000 when they died. They pay me about £7,500 a year, so I've saved them 80 years of my fees – pretty good value, I'd say (and so would they!).

There's obviously no way that I can adequately give you all the details you need to complete complex estate planning yourself in one small book. And there are so many wrinkles and quirks to the rules on pensions, estate planning, trusts and tax, that to include them all would make this book impenetrable and useless to you.

So I would urge you to seek professional advice. If you are in a position where you are likely to have an IHT problem, then you can afford to seek advice. Indeed, not to seek advice would be a false economy.

If you want to take your own planning further, perhaps as a precursor to seeking advice, then perhaps check out retirement planning courses online.

Chapter 21
Conclusion – A Meaningful Retirement

AS I WRITE THIS CONCLUSION, I'm thinking back to the hours I have spent writing this book. I have found the process much more difficult than my first book, not least because I was constantly having to decide what to include and what to leave out.

I believe that what I have covered in this book is enough for the vast majority of ordinary people to plan and execute their perfect retirement, to make sure that their later life is secure and to plan the transfer of wealth to their family.

I have omitted lots of detail, not because I want to keep it to myself, but so that it doesn't muddy the waters and get in the way of you being able to take action.

I hope it has been helpful.

Here at the end, I would like to encourage you to remember one thing above all else.

> Life is precious. Life is good. Life can be very enjoyable. Life is fleeting.

This life is not a rehearsal – we get one shot at it. If we are lucky enough to be able to retire with financial security, then enjoying life to the full should be our highest priority.

The great thing is that what constitutes a meaningful retirement is unique to each of us and we get to design our life as we wish, as long as we have the financial means to do so.

When I set out, I wanted to call this book 'A Meaningful Retirement'. My excellent editor Craig convinced me that the danger in that was that people might pick up the book thinking that it was about determining that meaning.

Instead, I hope that I have given you the practical tools to keep money in its place and to control it, so that you can get on with determining for yourself what a Meaningful Retirement looks like.

I wish you a long, happy and healthy retirement.

How I can help you further

We would love to talk to you at my financial planning firm, Jacksons. Head over to **jacksons.life** to see how we work and get in touch.

I also offer the Meaningful Academy retirement planning course. At Meaningful Academy you get tons of video lessons and workbooks to help you. You also get a year's access to the incredible financial planning software that I use every day with clients, plus I'll teach you how to use it.

Head over to **meaningfulacademy.com** and if you decide to sign up, use the coupon code BOOKTWO for a discount.

Endnotes

1 Jacksons is my financial planning practice in Penzance, Cornwall, UK. Check us out at jacksons.life.

2 Check him out at mrmoneymustache.com.

3 www.mrmoneymustache.com/2018/10/05/the-fire-movement.

4 Source: Carehome.co.uk, January 2024.

5 Source: NHS Digital Health Survey for England, 2021.

6 Source: ONS Life Expectancy in Care Homes, England and Wales 2021 to 2022.

7 Source: Office for National Statistics – 2020 Cohort, UK.

8 Source: Bank of England Inflation calculator.

9 Check out George Kinder's work at kinderinstitute.com.

10 www.moneyhelper.org.uk/en/pensions-and-retirement/pension-problems/tracing-and-finding-lost-pensions.

11 www.gov.uk/new-state-pension/what-youll-get.

12 www.gov.uk/check-state-pension.

13 meaningfulmoney.tv/pensiontracing.

14 This is a process, usually using powerful software, that enables the financial planner to project your situation forward, build possible alternative scenarios and stress-test solutions. You should insist on this from any prospective planner.

15 This isn't always possible, but it is something to aim for.

16 commonslibrary.parliament.uk/research-briefings/cbp-9517.

17 cornerstonewealthadvisors.com/decision-rules-and-maximum-initial-withdrawal-rates.

18   www.moneyhelper.org.uk/en/pensions-and-retirement/taking-your-pension/compare-annuities.

19   Including one from 7IM that shows their cautious funds recovering within two years 97% of the time and their growth fund recovering within two years 95% of the time.

20   ifs.org.uk/publications/how-does-spending-change-through-retirement-0.

21   Source: gov.uk.

22   www.hl.co.uk/tools/calculators/inheritance-tax-calculator.